ENDORSEMENTS

The Esther Mantle will awaken a fresh bravery in you! In just the first chapter, I was even more convicted that I must stand in this hour or miss what I was born to do at this moment in history. The alternative is to lose an entire generation to the devil—unacceptable! Friend, you are an Esther. Why not YOU? Why not NOW? This book will charge you to lay aside fear and excuses that stand in your way. It's time to pick up your Esther mantle!

Jenny L. Donnelly
Her Voice Mvmt, Founder

The book in your hand is a blueprint and a battle roar for the body of Christ to not be silent and bullied by the spirit of Haman, which has crept into the church our culture our nation and the nations of the world. In this book, Christy invites us to re-look at the book of Esther and see that we must contend for the personal mountain that God has called us to individually take a stand on. These are places that God has entrusted us to fill with light, for we, like Esther, have each been called for such a time as this!

Christy Johnson is a trusted friend and a gift to the body of Christ. She carries a prophetic voice and revelation on the power of the blood of Jesus to defeat the spirit of Haman that is essential in the times we are heading into! I have seen Christy walk these truths out in her personal life as well as her public life, and I am convinced that *The Esther Mantle* will help equip you to join her and others like her who have said "yes" to the Father's call in this pivotal moment in history!

Folake Kellogg
The Collective, Cashmere WA

We live in a culture with so many voices, opinions, and narratives that are desperately trying to destroy the image of women. Could it be that in this exact moment, God is rising up women across the globe to call a generation back to God? I believe this book will give spiritual and practical keys to every woman in our generation. May we live our lives challenged in the same way Esther was: for such a time as this.

Ross Johnston
Revivalist, California Will Be Saved

the ESTHER mantle

DESTINY IMAGE BOOKS BY CHRISTY JOHNSTON

*The Deborah Mantle: A Woman's Call to Arise
and Slay the Giants of Her Generation*

Releasing Prophetic Solutions

AN **URGENT CALL** FOR WOMEN TO STAND
AND **SHAPE HIS-TORY**

the
ESTHER
Mantle

CHRISTY JOHNSTON

DESTINY IMAGE® PUBLISHERS, INC.
P.O. Box 310, Shippensburg, PA 17257-0310

"Publishing cutting-edge prophetic resources to supernaturally empower the body of Christ"

This book and all other Destiny Image and Destiny Image Fiction books are available at Christian bookstores and distributors worldwide.

For more information on foreign distributors, call 717-532-3040.

Reach us on the Internet: www.destinyimage.com.

ISBN 13 TP: 978-0-7684-7725-2

ISBN 13 eBook: 978-0-7684-7726-9

For Worldwide Distribution, Printed in the U.S.A.

1 2 3 4 5 6 7 8 / 28 27 26 25 24

DEDICATION

To Natalie: You are every part a Queen Esther, and God has anointed you to lead your loved ones and your generation out of darkness and into the light of Jesus. I am honored to be your Aunty, and I am so proud of you.

For my daughters and to every daughter, young and old:

May you walk in Esther's mantle and proclaim Jesus to the ends of the earth. All of heaven is cheering you on.

CONTENTS

Foreword by Lou Engle 11

Introduction 15

PART ONE: THE ESTHER CALLING **19**

1   A *Kairos* Moment 21

2   Vashti Must Fall 47

3   Your Coronation 63

PART TWO: THE ESTHER CROWNING **83**

4   The Cost of the Call 85

5   A Star in the Night 103

6   Thorns to Crowns 123

PART THREE: THE ESTHER STRATEGY **143**

7   A Multitude of Noise 145

8   Rend the Heavens. 167

9   War at the Table 187

PART FOUR: THE ESTHER VICTORY **209**

10   Atonement. 211

11   Esther's Decree. 235

12   End-Time Victory 259

      About Christy Johnston 285

FOREWORD

Revelational! Inspirational! Incarnational! These words describe what I've experienced reading *The Esther Mantle* by our dear prophetic friend and intercessor Christy Johnston.

Revelational: I've read the book of Esther in the Bible many times, but my eyes have never seen some of the secret, mind-blowing treasures unfolded in these pages. The revelation of the Passover and Day of Atonement in the book of Esther are not readily evident to the casual observer, but, whoa—there they are and in many ways are the key to the sudden reversal. Talking to Nate, her husband and my friend, he described Christy's days of fasting and separation while digging for revelation, researching history, language, and meaning of words. Like Esther, Christy has served readers a banquet of rich foods and wine that will ultimately hang the antichrist Haman on his own gallows. They overcame him by the Blood of the Lamb. It's the Great Communion Revival at the end of the age.

Inspirational: I wept several times coursing over these pages. At the time of this writing, I'm mobilizing a vision of a million Esthers and Mordecais at the US National Mall on the Day of Atonement in possibly a last-stand cry for mercy for America. Who would not be inspired? I've found my name and my DNA written in *The Esther Mantle*. It is a present, throbbing personal prophecy to me, and it will be to you too if you are willing to risk everything to seize your own divine moment.

The Esther Mantle is not just a book but a divine summons to the church that demands a response. Esther is America's "now" book. Haman's destructive ideologies—death, transgenderism, censuring the voice of the righteous, and we-are-coming-for-your-kids' wickedness—pound relentlessly at the gates of America's death and destiny. Who would have guessed that at the releasing of *The Esther Mantle* a worldwide spirit of Haman in Hamas would manifest so violently. There are moments when chronos times collide, as Christy Johnston writes, with kairos epic moments when powerful, wealthy, evil men carrying their evil ideologies boast their seeming invincible dominion of the world; when the unseen dancing hand of providence overrules the arrogant; when immigrant exiles become the hinge of history; when orphans become queens; when sudden divine reversals interrupt the seeming irreversible flow of fate in history. We are in that collision of times.

The book of Esther trumpets throughout time and eternity that individuals (Mordecai's refusal to bow) and the church at large are not at the mercy of demonic and political decrees of destruction. Jesus is the Lord of history. God is the One who overrides the decrees of man and the church; even His Esthers are the agents of righteous revolution overthrowing kings and their decrees by the weapons of fasting and prayer and their "If I die I die" public confrontation of evil. Christy, you have inspired me greatly because the book is…

Incarnational: Your whole life story is an Esther story. She is in you and you in her. I wept reading your prophecies and dreams and stand in awe of the timings of those encounters. I'm moved by your boldness and roar in confronting evil and how God has backed you up in the most remarkable ways. I'm thrilled that God called you, one from another country like Esther, to fight for my country like the Australian Light Horse troops fought for Jerusalem. Roe v. Wade is no more because you among many listened to your Mordecai Jesus when He commanded you to risk all, move to America, and stand against abortion. Great leaders and writers give articulation to what is being groaned in the masses and thereby help stir mass moments and movements that shift history. Christy, your *Esther Mantle* is that kind of articulation for such a time as this.

Thank you!
Lou Engle

INTRODUCTION

I set out writing this book, seeking answers within Esther's profound victories for the issues we are facing in our day. I asked the Lord, "Would You please show me Your divine solutions for the problems around us? Would You highlight the spiritual weaponry within the book of Esther, and help me to understand how to wield the strategies You gave her in our day?" My desire in writing *The Esther Mantle,* has been to pass on a battle plan to you, daughter, as you carry Esther's mantle into the darkest places of the earth and culture. For, it does not take a prophet to recognize that the hour at hand is one of critical peril.

We stand in a moment of time, perhaps unlike any before us. While I recognize every age has faced its own dangers, chaos, wars, and societal upheaval, ours is a tumult dissimilar to any before it. We are witnessing, in real time, the dismantling of every design of God. From the family unit, to marriage, to the identities of children as males and females. Our children are being plagued with ideologies of boundless "sex identities"—sexuality is being pushed on them at alarming rates, they are under assault in schools not only through shootings, but teachings as well.

The agenda to confuse and bewilder innocent young minds, convincing them that males can be females and females can be males is perhaps the most aggressive and egregious of our time. The mere word *female* has become a word of contention, and young girls are losing their safety and rights within bathrooms and on the sporting fields. As if that is not enough, the ongoing battleground of the womb is by far the most vicious and bloodthirsty fight of all. If we could see the blood of the millions of babies that have been sacrificed, it would fill the streets as blood rivers.

We are also faced with insidious corruption within government—the exposure of pedophilia rings within both government and Hollywood. Sexual perversion is infiltrating policymaking with the attempt of pedophilic bills being pushed into states, with California as just one example, that would eliminate the age of sexual consent for minors. And then, of course, are the bills that would sanction state-owned children, removing parents from the equation of decision-making over their very own offspring.

Horrific wars and rumors of wars, not to mention the explosive opinions surrounding these wars. Within churches, we are witnessing the rise of "deconstruction" and a vast falling away of believers.

Need I go on? What will come of tomorrow if we do nothing today? Where does this leave us? What is the answer?

My vision for this book was to write a spiritual weapon to put in your hands—and the prayer I prayed, asking the Lord to give me a battle plan, was answered in a way I never expected. As I began studying Esther, I found incredible, hidden messages that

I had never seen or noticed before. Perhaps, they were concealed until this moment within her story for this hour of great need. The answers the Holy Spirit led me to, brought me to my knees. I've cried more tears in writing *The Esther Mantle* than any book before it. Not tears of sorrow, but tears of awe and wonder. From the very first chapter of Esther, you are about to discover, Jesus is written all throughout it. While there is no distinct mention of Him, He is there in every detail, and it is truly astounding. From beginning to end, we will together find the answer for the hour we are in is none other than Jesus.

It's all about the Lamb.

PART ONE

the ESTHER Calling

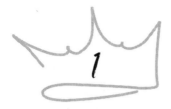

A *KAIROS* MOMENT

BIBLE READING: ESTHER 1:1-13

4:14

"There it is again!"

I shouted to myself as I noticed the precise hour and minute of 4:14 in the afternoon. It was early 2019, and no matter what I was doing each day, my eyes would somehow, mysteriously, be drawn to look at the clock on my wall, or at the time on my phone, at exactly fourteen minutes past the hour of four o'clock.

I found myself waking suddenly at 4:14 a.m. in the early hours of the dawn as the sun broke through the night across the horizon. And let me tell you, I'm not a morning person, so this was highly unusual for me. My eyes would later fall upon the time on our oven at exactly 4:14 p.m. as the afternoon sun slowly yawned into the dusk of evening. No matter what I was doing, I was being drawn to this exact moment of time each day.

I then began noticing 414 in other places too, including 414 likes or comments on one of my Instagram posts. And $4.14 etched on the receipt of a morning coffee. Or 414 unread emails (oh, how I loathe an inbox overflowing with junk mail). I would find myself sitting impatiently in traffic, only to notice I was stuck behind a car with 414 as part of the license plate. We even bought a car in early 2020, and of all the cars we found, the one we picked just happened to have 414 on the license plate registration. I would be driving somewhere and my arrival time on the map would be exactly 4:14 p.m.

Regardless of what I was doing each day, 414 was becoming a daily repetition, and I knew it was the Holy Spirit drawing me to Esther 4:14. Yet I didn't fully grasp the gravity of what the Lord was saying. I wondered to myself, *Is this verse self-explanatory, or is there is something deeper the Lord wants to show me?*

As I write, the year is 2024, and to this day, 414 is a regular occurrence, whether noticing the minute and hour on my phone or happening upon it in some other way. In fact, just this morning, my sister who lives in Australia sent me a text asking for prayer over her and her younger daughter, the time stamp on the text she sent was 4:14 a.m.

I wonder, have you noticed this too? The strange phenomenon of catching the clock at the exact same time each day? Have you been noticing 4:14 as well? If not, I can guarantee you of this, you will now. By reading this book, you have signed yourself up for this mantle, so be prepared for the Lord to inundate your days with His clarion call from Heaven.

This isn't a happenstance; it is the Holy Spirit drawing you and me to attention to the hour at hand. We are in a time like no other, a time of urgency and calling. A time when the Lord is ushering His voice like a trumpet from Heaven, with zeal He is crying out,

"If you keep silent at this time, relief and deliverance will come to the Jewish people from another place, but you and your father's family will be destroyed. Who knows, perhaps you have come to your royal position for such a time as this" (Esther 4:14 CSB). Upon reading this verse, you may be asking, "Keep silent from 'what' precisely?" Is this only regarding the Jewish people and was this call to attention reserved for their time alone—or is there a broader message here, to us, the Gentile in our modern day as well?

The verse in 2 Timothy 3:16 (ESVUK) tells us that *"All Scripture is breathed out by God and profitable for teaching, for reproof, for correction, and for training in righteousness."* God did not write verse, chapter, and stories throughout the Bible to leave it merely in the time it was written, these Scriptures are provided to speak to us, teach us, and train us in the context for our day today.

So what is the warning to us specifically in Esther 4:14? What is it we could be silent from in our day that threatens to engulf our lives and families if we stand on the sidelines and say nothing? I believe it is our silence in opposing the spiritual war on our children and the coming generations. The silence of speaking out about the evils of our day. Silence from the spirit of Haman that has descended like a thick cloud upon our earth. If we remain silent, there is no future for us or our children.

A dear friend of mine shared with me a dream she recently had, which I felt was so powerfully poignant to this message that I just had to share it with you as well. My friend, Folake Kellogg, a dreamer and prophetic voice, heard the Lord speak to her in this dream, where He said, "You cannot have Esther 4:14 without Nehemiah 4:14." When she awoke, she read the scripture the Lord had shared with her which says:

And I looked, and rose up, and said unto the nobles, and to the rulers, and to the rest of the people, Be not ye afraid of them: remember the Lord, which is great and terrible, and fight for your brethren, your sons, and your daughters, your wives, and your houses (**Nehemiah 4:14 KJV**).

If you are familiar with the story of Nehemiah, you will know that the walls of Jerusalem had been broken down, its gates in ruins, its people plundered. Nehemiah was a Jewish exile living in Persia (the very place where Esther's story plays out) and he was a cupbearer to the king. When he heard of the news, he was distraught and resolved to do something about it.

In Nehemiah 2, an interesting conversation plays out between Nehemiah and the king, who had noticed his esteemed cup-bearer was visibly distressed. He asked Nehemiah what it was that he wanted. In Nehemiah 2:6 (CSB) we read, "The king, with the queen seated beside him, asked me, 'How long will your journey take, and when will you return?' So I gave him a definite time, and it pleased the king to send me."

I did some research on this verse and discovered something amazing. It appears that the very king we read of in Esther is the same king in Nehemiah. Furthermore, these two books of the Bible, Esther and Nehemiah, are not in chronological order as they appear in the lineup of the 66 books within our Bible. Therefore, the story of Esther actually came first. Furthermore, upon deeper inspection and study upon dates and times, the queen mentioned in Nehemiah 2 is indeed Queen Esther.

What is the lesson here? Esther was key in rebuilding the broken-down walls of homes, families and children. Without her taking up her position, a Persian queen would have likely been seated at the king's side in her place in this critical moment. A Persian queen who would have had no interest in helping God's people rebuild and restore. Instead, God divinely positioned Esther, a Jewish queen who had favor with the king. We know her for the marvelous story we recount from her book, but she is integral to Nehemiah as well. Without her favor with the king, it's likely he would have never allowed his cupbearer to leave his side to rebuild the walls of his hometown. Instead, he not only sends Nehemiah, but gives him the tools to do so.

Folake's dream tells us that without the daughters of God arising in this hour, there is no rebuilding of the walls of our broken-down homes, families and cities. The mantle of Esther is integral to the hour at hand.

TIMES OF TENSION

I believe we have romanticized, in many ways, much of Esther's story, and those infamous words of her uncle Mordecai. We love to wear t-shirts with his renowned catchphrase, *"for such a time as this,"* and I'll be the first to say, I own one of those, so I have nothing against them. I only want to emphasize that *"for such a time as this"* is perhaps more crucial in our own day than we have previously given thought to.

The entire book of Esther speaks of tension and transition, struggle and triumph, fear and faith. What does that really look like though? And, how can we compare with her struggle in our own lives? It's easy to disassociate from Esther's wrestle when we have thousands of years between her story and our own—not to mention the vast cultural differences between Persia and the West from then and now.

We tend to give heavy focus on her glorious triumph, without deeply considering her tears. If she was alive in our time what would her tears be pouring over? When we are in the thick of trial and tension, do any of us really cry out gleefully, "Yay, I'm in my Esther 4:14 moment!" I can't think of anyone who responds in that way. Personally, I wail and cry, I have times of wrestling with the Lord, asking Him, "Do You see what I'm dealing with here? This doesn't feel fair."

Esther's story is one of difficult strain, but the pressure she endures is necessary for the measure of what is drawn out of her—courage, hope, purpose, strength, and resilience. I want you to consider the trials of our world today and ask, "What would God have called Esther to contend for in our day?" Then, in the context of your own personal life, as God mantles you with this anointing of Esther's, ask again, "Father, what are You specifically calling me to contend for in my life and world?"

You see, daughter, you may be facing a trial right now, wondering, *What am I doing here? How did I get here?* I want to ask you, will you allow me to speak into your life for a moment? You see, my heart is to encourage you throughout this book, but you need to know something about me, I'm not going to lather you with words that just tickle your ears. I'm going to pull you up higher; I'm going to speak into the daughter of strength that you are and call the gold from within your spirit. Allow me to prophesy over you for a moment: This trial you may be in will not be able to break you because God has positioned you, for such a time as this. Yes, this hour in which you are living *is* your Esther 4:14 moment. It may not feel like it, it may not look like it, it may feel more like a struggle than a triumph. Yet I am here to remind you of the Father's promise over you, through my own testimony, that you *will* prevail over everything the enemy sends your way. You are *strong* in the Lord and in His mighty power (Ephesians 6:10).

TIMES OF TRANSITION

I want to share with you a little snippet of our own journey. A time when we were in the middle of one "for such a time as this" moment and yet, we didn't even realize it in the present. The struggle and the tension were not just difficult, it was like a tearing, a painful separation from the old, into the new. My husband, Nate, and I, along with our children have moved seven times in the past four years, not all by preferred choice I will add. I am a homebody through and through. I love to feel settled, and one of my favorite hobbies is home design. I love nothing more than creating a beautiful, peaceful environment for my family.

Consequently, moving as often as we have has been profoundly distressing on my heart. I've had to learn to lean into the Lord as my comfort in ways I had never encountered Him previously. I can confidently say we understand the pains of transition better than most. The process of gaining our visas for the United States was a tumultuous ride of ups and downs.

Covid disrupted our visa application process, delaying us by two years and causing us to move around as we waited. Our visa application was initially rejected on baseless grounds, and we had to apply again, setting us right back to the beginning. After more months of delay, we finally secured an appointment with the US consulate in Sydney, Australia. Two weeks prior to that appointment, we received a notification that the US Consulate was closing for refurbishment, with no given time frame of when it would reopen, or how we could reapply. The setbacks and delay were distressing.

Nate and I found ourselves constantly before the Lord, seeking His direction and timing. While back in Australia during the year 2022, in what would be the final phase of awaiting our visas, the confusion was the greatest we have ever faced. Prophetic words were given to us on nearly a daily basis. I use the word *prophetic* loosely here, as in hindsight, these words sounded prophetic, but were "soulish" words. Meaning, they were spoken out of people's souls—their mind, will, and emotions—rather than hearing the voice of the Spirit of God. Words like, "If you go to America, you are forfeiting and aborting what God has called you to here in Australia," were the most common. Those words played on our heart strings.

We deeply love our homeland and pray for her and our people; however, we could not deny what God was calling us to in this season of time. It was a mind-warfare that we had to walk through each day. We questioned, "Are we doing the right thing?" "Are we subjecting our children to endless warfare because we're following what we believe to be the Lord for all of our lives?" "Why is nothing working when God called us to this, maybe we're wrong?" "Maybe we are aborting the calling to our own nation?"

Every time these questions were raised in our minds, we had to position ourselves in the quiet before the Lord—away from the noise. We would seek His face and inquire, "Lord, remind us again. Tell us what YOU say." Each time, His counsel would direct us, "I have called you and your family for a time to the nation of the United States of America." Whenever I saw the number 4:14 jump out at me each day, I would be constantly reminded of that, perhaps, He was calling us to this nation for such a time as this. Not because we're anything special, but because we knew if we didn't, we and our children may perish. Maybe not physically, but spiritually. We would be sacrificing our comforts for the sake of His calling, and we could not do that.

The Father also reminded us of a word spoken over us many years ago, "I am sending you out as a boomerang." We never understood it then, but today I do. Boomerangs are weapons for the aboriginal community, and I understand now that by surrendering to the Lord's will and His ways, by sending us out, He would one day send us back, and in the meantime, He would send spiritual weaponry and awakening to our home country of Australia.

The number of times we have come to a place of wanting to give up on our visas and the call of God to position ourselves in the US is more times than I can remember. Living in the in-between was a painful place to be. We were neither here, nor there. We couldn't commit to things like buying our children a puppy because we didn't know where we were going to be living from one moment to the next.

When our visas finally did come through and we ultimately made it to the United States, we faced yet another test of opposition. Upon landing from our long 17-hour flight from Sydney to Dallas in January 2023, we were weary beyond comprehension. Not only from our flight, but from the years of warfare leading up to this moment.

As we waited in the three-hour-long custom lines, three tired children in tow, we finally made it to the end, anxiously anticipating getting out of the airport and driving to our new home. I was dreaming of taking a nice hot shower and collapsing into our beds that dear friends had helped set up in preparation for our arrival.

However, the customs officer took one stern look at us and asked us to follow him. My heart sank. He led us to an examining room filled with at least 150 people before us, and, without any explanation, he slammed the door and locked it behind us. The room was overflowing with no spare seats to sit on, so we huddled next to a Coca-Cola vending machine and sat on the dirty floor. If you can picture in your mind the worst DMV office you can imagine, or for our Aussie friends, a state transport office with hundreds of people, men, women, and children, packed in like sardines with your number being the very last after a 17-hour flight and three-hour customs line, you can imagine our despair.

I was growing claustrophobic and could feel panic setting in over my mind, I kept thinking, *Where am I going to get food for my older girls and little toddler?* Ava, only two at the time, had eaten almost everything I had packed for the long-haul flight, and I only had a snack or two remaining. With just one vending machine filled only with sodas, my mind was reeling.

Nate approached the front desk, handing over our passports, and he was told, "You could be here another ten hours, get comfortable." We knew this was the enemy attempting to discourage and stop us from crossing into the promised land that God had led us to, the United States of America. I will admit to you, satan had done a pretty good job of doing so; we felt defeated and intimidated. Everything within me just wanted to run back to Australia. Our children began weeping, exhausted from the journey, and now, with no clear end in sight, they were hungry and tired, with no food available.

So we did all we knew to do, we sat together in a circle, with the whole room seemingly listening in, as we desperately prayed to the Lord, "God, if ever we have needed You, we need You now. Deliver us!" As we prayed together, Nate saw two angels in the spirit and heard the Lord say, "I have sent them to usher you out of there."

At that very moment, our names were called at the front desk, and almost like out of a dream, the man at the front desk who was previously cold and hard, now gently smiled. He looked at Nate and apologized, "Sir, I am so sorry. You should not have been sent in here, it was a mistake. I had this random thought come to my mind that I needed to check your passports, I never do that. I wouldn't have checked them for hours yet. Someone must be watching over you." At that, he handed Nate our passports, buzzed the door open (like a prison cell) and released us.

We walked out of there with tears streaming down all our faces, and we could physically feel the presence of God ushering us out. We turned to our girls and said, "You just witnessed Jesus moving on our behalf." We were all crying tears of relief as we ran to the baggage claim to retrieve our bags. Ours were the last ones to be taken from the flight, sitting all alone in the middle of the baggage carousel.

What's even more miraculous about that moment was that no sooner had we walked out of that holding area, within mere minutes, there was a nationwide system failure in the processing computers. Everyone who was in that room, and likewise in customs, was sadly trapped there for an additional 24 hours. It truly felt like our own "crossing of the Red Sea" with just seconds behind us before utter chaos broke out.

All to say, the process of surrendering to transition, when all around you feels out of control, is possibly one of the most difficult times you can walk through. Yet you can be sure of this: He who promised to lead you through the transition is faithful to guide you to the end.

A WORLD IN TENSION AND TRANSITION

I am reminded of our own transition as I look at the world around us.

The culture of our day is in rapid transition. Confusion is abounding, and a ruckus of turbulent opinions and "my truths" have filled the streets. It is difficult to determine what is real and what is not. We are in a place of neither here, nor there, for there is a vicious spiritual wrestle for the human mind as foundational truths are contested in the public square. We will investigate in later chapters of this book, just what is behind this tension.

The definition of *transition* from Oxford Language is "the process or a period of changing from one state or condition to another." I would suggest that they should add within that definition the pain and discomfort that is presented within change. I find it relatively ironic that the word *transition* has become somewhat of a buzz word and trend in today's culture. Though the transition our culture speaks of is the attempted process of transforming one's gender identity into something it is not and never can be, ultimately it is the enemy's divisive attempt to remove and replace God's perfect design.

Notice how the same symptoms abound? Bewilderment, confusion, false prophecy (or rather, false prediction and promise of outcome: noisy statements such as, "You will be happier once you transition." These statements drown out the reality of truth over vulnerable children and youth).

Furthermore, there is the havoc and disorder that such transition brings. Biological men competing in women's sports for just one example. Considering all this, and with the hindsight of our own story in mind, I wonder, *Could it be that transition attracts warfare for a reason? Could it be that our world is in transition, on the border of mass revival and awakening, and the enemy knows it? What is he seeing that we cannot?*

Much like our time sitting in the examining room at the airport, the enemy is trying to throw all he has at this generation because he knows what it will cost him when they cross the border and meet the Lord. Could this generation, one that has been bombarded with messages of transition and confusion, be the very generation that ushers in the long-awaited promises of God's outpouring over the earth?

I am reminded of a quote by our dear friend, Lou Engle:

> There are moments in history when a door for massive change opens, and great revolutions for good or evil spring up in the vacuum created by these openings. In these divine moments key men and women and even entire generations risk everything to become the hinge of history, the pivotal point that determines which way the door will swing.

I wholeheartedly believe we are finding ourselves in such a moment. Is it possible that the outcome of this transition rests, dare I say, solely upon the response of the body of Christ? The ecclesia. I believe so. What if, just what if, we were a people who did not hide from the discomforts of our day, but like that moment on the floor in the examining room, in desperation, we cried out as one, "God, if ever we needed You, it's now! Deliver us! Deliver Your people."

I truly believe we are in a moment of opportunity, whereby the Lord is calling upon His bride saying, "Will you seize this moment of divine opportunity to discern the times and respond as Esther did? Or will you succumb to the noise of the age, the chaos and confusion of Haman and surrender your calling for the sake of comfort and the avoidance of disruption? Will you run in moments of discomfort, or will you seek My face? Will you listen to the false prophets, the ones who speak out of their soul and cry out in the public square, 'Love is love, you can do whatever you please, Jesus doesn't care. God loves abortion. God is a she. There is no such thing as hell.'"

Or will you hold fast to the infallible truth of God's word, that cries out in the streets, like John the Baptist: "Repent, for the

Kingdom of Heaven is at hand! Prepare the way of the Lord!" Will you pursue the enemy principality of Haman in our day, principalities that are working with Haman, the sound of whom fills the airwaves, intimidating and mocking God's truth? Transition, my friend, is no walk in the park. Yet, at what cost is the alternative? I believe we are standing on the precipice of either a great outpouring or a great depression.

Mordecai's somber words in Esther 4:14 warn us clearly: *"You and your father's family will perish."* I don't share these words to elicit fear, for God has given us hope for this hour; yet, the warning is impossible to ignore. We must step into the mantle of Esther—for if we choose comfort over calling, the cost is grave. While the plans of this principality of Haman in our day may not be a physical decree of death (although, I would argue that there are physical consequences through the likes of abortion for example), we face a multitude of noise, a spiritual army of darkness that is attempting to devour the minds of our children, their identities, and the future of our children's children. One need not have children to take up this mantle—this is a call for every son and every daughter, irrespective of age, status, or parental position. God is calling us as one Bride to step into the mantle of Esther for the perilous hour at hand.

THE HOUR IS URGENT

The entire kingdom of Persia was thrown into upheaval through the dismissive actions of Queen Vashti. I've read multiple commentaries about Vashti, and I have come to notice that there are two distinct camps of perception concerning her. One camp lauds proudly over her actions, declaring her a "feminist boss" of her time by denying the king his request of her presence before all the nobles. Others are not so impressed and conclude that her denial was necessary for the Lord to position Esther. I am of the latter camp, and I intend to delve further into her story and explain why that is my understanding later.

For now, however, I propose this thought: Vashti chose comfort over calling. Admittedly, her calling was to stand beside her king as an exaltation to his wealth and magnificence. I admit, I do feel torn about her, for I perceive that her dismissal was because of the king's drunkenness. Perhaps she felt she would be ridiculed and laughed at. I empathize with her for that reason, but it brings me to a conclusion that represents you and me in this moment.

I question, what if there was something that the king wanted to gift Vashti in front of all the nobles? He offered so with Esther—"*Whatever you want, even to half the kingdom, will be given to you*" (Esther 5:3 CSB)—when she appeared before him. So, it seemed the king was in high and generous spirits. He had been lavishly displaying his wealth to his entire kingdom—what if he had wanted to gift Vashti with something? A position of greater authority, more territory? It's just a thought, I know, but upon much examination of her story, it is something I do speculate about.

Despite my empathy for Vashti, her position and calling required of her to respond to her king; therefore, her response was indeed selfish and arrogant. She chose her own comfort to avoid the discomfort of the king's request. Thus, she was swiftly and rightly removed.

Vashti's actions are a warning to us today. God is calling forth his daughters in this hour to stand in places of prominence. Is it possible we will find those places humiliating or uncomfortable? Will we be ridiculed for our stand? Will we be laughed at and rejected by the masses? It's likely.

Yet, our own King's decree is calling, and we cannot ignore Him for the sake of comfort—we must respond, no matter the cost. While King Ahasuerus is no King Jesus by any means; he represents realms of earthly authority, for his name means "chief." The Greek version of his name that many Bible translations use is *Xerxes* and means "monarch, brave and strong, ruler of heroes." Could this earthly king represent earthly government? He was far from perfect, but I believe he prophetically speaks of God's favor being bestowed upon His sons and daughters in this hour in the high places of authority in modern civilization. The church has long disengaged in the public square, and I believe the Lord is bringing us back to pour out Truth and healing upon all sectors of society.

CALLING OVER COMFORT

Vashti's removal triggered immediate transition in the Persian kingdom, a snowball-type effect that impacted many, especially the young unmarried women, namely that of young Esther. I imagine she would have been led away from her home at a moment's notice. I often think of her in that unsettling transition—what was it like for her to be taken from the safety of her home and the protective arms of her uncle, Mordecai, almost definitely against her will. I can only imagine that her dreams of a normal life crashed behind her.

Incidentally, I'm jumping ahead of her story here, but I want to highlight the famous charge of Mordecai from Esther 4:14 (NIV). His words are full of somber weightiness and urgency for the task she faced. Esther was thrust from her quiet life into a place of prominence that demanded a courageous response from her.

> *For if you remain silent at this time, relief and deliverance for the Jews will arise from another place, but you and your father's family will perish. And who knows but that you have come to your royal position for such a time as this?*

Was Esther finding herself in a full-circle moment of redemption where Vashti's abdication of responsibility was now being handed to her to fulfill? Had all the uncomfortable transition she faced—the loss of her parents at a young age, living in exile in a foreign land, being taken from her home and now finding herself queen of that foreign land—led to this one critical juncture of time? Indeed.

I want to draw your attention to a word mentioned twice in this verse. For God is not careless in Scripture, every word is written with distinct purpose, and I want to highlight the word *time* that Mordecai speaks here on two occasions. *"For if you remain silent at this time"* and *"for such a time as this."* The word *time* described here, is the Hebrew word *eth* and means "interval, time, a period, mealtime, season, year, appointed time, circumstance." What's interesting about this word is it speaks of both *chronos* and *kairos* times.

Chronos and *kairos* are Greek terms used in the New Testament to denote two variations of the measure of time. *Chronos* speaks into the daily measure of time, the marching of each second as it ticks unceasingly into minutes and hours. *Chronos* is how we measure our days, it is the times and seasons, it is the ages and times of our lifetimes, the dash between a person's date of birth and date of death. *Chronos* is what measures the length of our time here on earth. Just as *eth* suggests it is a "time, period, and season."

Kairos, on the other hand, is a divine moment of time when God interrupts our time and intersects with moments of sudden visitation and divine interruption. We can see moments of *kairos* throughout the Bible and in history. In the Greek, *kairos* is described as "the right or critical moment." *Kairos* is extraordinary and supernatural time requiring interpretation and response, and it can also be described as moments of chaos and crisis. Crisis is often found within the midst of *kairos*. Why? Because as God comes close, the darkness manifests.

Allow me to show you some verses in Scripture where *chronos* and *kairos* are mentioned:

> *Pay careful attention, then, to how you walk, not as unwise but as wise, redeeming the **time**, because the days are evil. Therefore, do not be foolish, but understand what the Lord's will is. Do not get drunk on wine, which leads to reckless indiscretion. Instead, be filled with the Spirit* (**Ephesians 5:15-18 BSB**).

The word used for time in this verse is *kairos*. Pay attention to how you walk, redeeming the *kairos*—the appointed time and opportune moment.

Here is another verse where *kairos* is found. Read the word *time* as *kairos*, considering the urgency of the message:

> They will dash you to the ground, you and the children within your walls. They will not leave one stone on another, because you did not recognize the **time** of God's coming to you (**Luke 19:44 NIV**).

This verse from Luke reminds me of a New Testament version of Esther 4:14, but this verse shows us what will happen if we don't respond. Is it distressing? Yes, which is why we cannot be like Vashti in this moment and refuse to come before the King. We must lay down the cost before us and seize this moment, recognizing the *kairos* of God's coming to us. He is with us; and like Esther, He is our ever-present help in a time of need.

Now, let's look at *chronos:*

> But when the set **time** had fully come, God sent his Son, born of a woman, born under the law (**Galatians 4:4 NIV**).

The word used for *time* in this Galatians verse is *chronos*. There was a set time for Jesus to be born, and I find it fascinating that *chronos* is mentioned here and not *kairos*, because Jesus was a *kairos* moment. He was a collision of *kairos* into *chronos*. When the Holy Spirit came upon Mary's womb, it was God sovereignly invading our chronological time.

In a similar way, the Hebrew word *eth* is a collision of both *chronos* and *kairos*. It is both a moment of time and an appointed time. Could we be standing in a *chronos* of time when the divine *kairos* of God is crashing into our timeline? I believe so. It is my understanding that we are in *chronos* and *kairos* respectively. *Eth* is also derived from the word *anah,* which means "to answer or respond." It's imperative to understand that such a moment demands not only wisdom, led by the Holy Spirit, but also a response.

When Mordecai sent these words to Esther, notice that he demanded a response. Prior to this, she had waved him away, not wanting to engage in the tension of the moment—but Mordecai drew out of her the destiny within her. He summoned her attention to the critical season she was standing in, and the decision of life and death that she had to make. Esther thought herself separated from the issues facing her people—how many of us today have done the same? Could it be that God is calling upon you in this moment, and what's required may feel a little uncomfortable as you step out of your comfort zone? Yet, what is the alternative?

DISCERNING THE TIMES

In the New Testament, Jesus was constantly having altercations with the Pharisees. One consistent rebuke of His against them was their inability, or perhaps, their unwillingness to discern the times. If they were true followers of God, then surely they would have recognized Him to be the true Son of God. If not through His miracles, at the very least, they should have been able to determine they were standing right in a *kairos* moment of time, based alone on the prophecies surrounding the Messiah that offered details about the timing. However, for all their apparent wisdom and knowledge, they knew nothing, and Jesus rebuked them as such.

In Matthew 16:1-3 (BSB), a conversation ensues between the Pharisees and Jesus:

> *Then the Pharisees and Sadducees came and tested Jesus by asking Him to show them a sign from heaven. But He replied, "When evening comes, you say, 'The weather will be fair, for the sky is red,' and in the morning, 'Today it will be stormy, for the sky is red and overcast.' You know how to interpret the appearance of the sky, but not the signs of the times. A wicked and adulterous generation demands a sign, but none will be given it except the sign of Jonah." Then He left them and went away.*

The Greek word Jesus used for *times,* is indeed, *kairos.* This word can also mean "coming to a head." Could this warning stand for us today? I believe so. Everything around us is coming to a head, we are in a *kairos.* We are living amid a wicked and adulterous generation, and they too are demanding a sign, saying, "Show me your God is real. Give me proof that your 'sky Daddy' isn't some fictious character." What's alarming is that Jesus didn't distinguish that the Pharisees were any different from the wicked generation; but rather, gave the connotation that they were one and the same. Why? Because they didn't discern the times.

This tells me that not only *discerning* the times but *responding* to the times is of imperative importance. How so, you may ask. Jesus mentions Jonah in His rebuke to the Pharisees for a reason. Jonah was sent to a wicked city to call out the evil and then urge the people to turn away from their wickedness and turn back to God. Jesus mentioned Jonah here because His desire is that you and I would go out into the darkest places of the earth and compel people to repent and turn to Him, for the hour is short. It is His desire that no one perish.

Yet the Pharisees did not care for the lost, they cared only for their reputation. The sign of Jonah would be that without repentance, destruction would come. A *kairos* demands our discernment and our response. We cannot sit idly by while the world around us is on the pathway to hell. We cannot be like the Pharisees who were only concerned with themselves. They ask, "What good will it do if I help anyone? Isn't the Messiah supposed to be returning soon, anyway? I'll just wait for Him to beam me up." The warning here is that God does not look kindly on our inability to discern the times, nor on our choosing not to respond.

When Jesus instructed us to "occupy" until He comes in Luke 19:13 (KJV), He was telling us to "get to work." The Greek word for *occupy* is *pragmateuomai,* which means "to busy oneself with a necessary matter, to make exchange, to trade, and to make gain." Occupy is the opposite of being fruitless by choosing to play it safe. This is not an hour to play it safe, this is an hour in which to fully engage, and we must exchange the darkness for the Light.

Interestingly, when Vashti was deposed, the king turned to his wise counsel. The upheaval and transition of time demanded wise discernment and a response. Esther 1:13 (BSB) tells us: *"Then the king consulted the wise men who knew the times, for it was customary for him to confer with the experts in law and justice."* Upon reading this, I knew there was something more in the messaging, so I began to study into the name meanings of the wise men. What I found was initially perplexing. Almost every name has a double meaning. Then I realized the names of the wise men themselves point to two differing messages: *"His closest advisors were Carshena, Shethar, Admatha, Tarshish, Meres, Marsena, and Memucan, the seven princes of Persia and Media who had personal access to the king and ranked highest in the kingdom"* (Esther 1:14 BSB).

Carshena means a lamb and sleeping. Shethar means searching and despised. Admatha means a testimony to them, and a cloud of death or mortal vapor. Tarshish means white dove, searching for alabaster, courage, subjection, and breaking. Meres means a boundary and defluxion or imposthume. Marsena simply means bitterness of a bramble. And Memucan means certain and true.

What I drew from their name meanings are two different scenarios. One is speaking of the *awake and alert bride* that carries the Lamb; like John the Baptist, she is the one crying out in the wilderness, "repent, prepare the way of the Lord." The other is the *sleeping bride.* Collectively, I've pieced together like a puzzle the meanings of their names for the awake bride. This is what the Holy Spirit led me to write through the names of the wise men that discerned the times: "She is searching for the lost, declaring a *testimony to them;* with *courage* she cries out at the *boundaries* of the city square; look to the *Lamb,* the One caught in the *bitterness of a bramble* (the lamb caught in the thicket from Genesis 22:13, bramble and thicket are similar words), He is certain and true, your rescue."

Then there is the sleeping bride. She does not carry the Lamb to the lost, and thus her actions are *despised* of the Lord, just like the Pharisees. Her slumber allows a *cloud of death* and *a mortal vapor* to rest upon the earth around her. The wise men in these verses are, in essence, a warning and a picture of the parable of the ten virgins (Matthew 25:1-13). Five fell asleep when the hour was critical, and the other five went and bought oil. Is it any coincidence then, that the names of these wise men who discerned the times were prophetically pointing to Esther, and subsequently to you and me today?

Amazingly, one of the names also means "search for alabaster." In the coming chapters, I'll explain why this is so profound. They were prophetically anointed to search for the daughter, Esther, who would carry the sweet perfume of Jesus (albeit, a foreshadow of Him), to the kingdom around her. They were searching for the one who would carry the Lamb in a moment of time who needed discernment and response.

Daughter, you are that Esther—the *kairos* hour we are in is one of peril, and this is no time to sleep. This is the time to buy oil and to stand, and cry out as John the Baptist:

> *Behold, the Lamb of God, who takes away the sins of the world! Repent, for the Kingdom of heaven is at hand* (**John 1:29,36; Matthew 4:17; Matthew 12:41 ESVUK**).

This *kairos* hour declares: This the hour of the Lamb, for such a time as this.

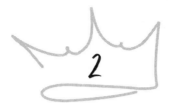

2

VASHTI MUST FALL

BIBLE READING: ESTHER 1:14-22

As we briefly disussed earlier, there are conflicting opinions about Vashti. Is she the damsel in distress, or the queen in rebellion? Many believe her ousting to be an unjust action from an unstable king. I believe we can find a clue into who she really is in the story by studying her name meaning and looking accordingly at the context of the Scriptures that mention her.

As Vashti was the queen of a Persian king, her name is a little difficult to transcribe. However, allow me to share this etymology of her name as it's translated into both Persian, or Arabic, and then the Hebrew language. Starting with the Persian, or Arabic, her name is derived from a word that means "beautiful one."

In Hebrew, this is translated from the noun *sheti*, which means "drinking," and from the verb *shata,* to "drink." I'm going to dig a little further to show you something fascinating through the Hebrew translation of her name. The verb *shata* is connected to the verb *sha'a*, which means to "roar loudly with destruction in mind." It can also point to the noun *sha'on*, which describes "the roaring sound of wild waters or armies converging." Additionally, the noun *sha'awa* denotes a "devastating storm." Nouns *she'iya* and *she't* means "ruin."

Upon reading these translations of Vashti's name, I immediately thought of a dream I had of a sea of women on the Washington Mall, which I will share in detail later in this chapter. In brief, a loud roar came out of my spirit, and then the roar of an army of women roared back at me, converging with mine. However, ours was not a roar that was destructive to those around us; rather, it was a loud roar that was devastating to the works of darkness.

This is fascinating—the etymology of Vashti's name points to the opposite spirit of Esther. Vashti's is a destructive and devastating storm that works against the plans of God. Esther's is one that works with the Lord. I must show you something else here. The Hebrew verb הוש or *shawa* can also mean "to be smooth and hence to agree with or to be like one another." The noun הוש *shaweh* describes "a level plain."

We have a cultural mindset in Australia known as "the tall poppy syndrome" that is worth mentioning in this context. This mindset identifies the nationwide phenomena of cutting down those who speak their minds. For example, if a person speaks their mind, raises their head above the rest of the crowd, or shows any level of difference, whether by success or thought and speech, they are like a tall poppy. The tall poppy represents a poppy flower in a field of poppies that has risen its head too high above the rest; and therefore, the other poppies seek to cut down the tall poppy.

For people who speak a different tone or voice, they are harshly cut down, belittled, and mocked by their fellow Australians. For that reason, as Australians, we have been largely conditioned to "be smooth and agreeable," to be like one another, not raise our heads, or get too big for our britches by thinking different from the rest.

The world watched Australia in shock during the lockdowns of 2020, where for the most part, our nation subserviently bowed to the overarching governmental restrictions set by officials drunk on power. I believe this happened in large part because of the tall poppy syndrome. Look at what happens to an entire country of people who have fallen prey to this mindset.

Vashti's name is derived from a verb that means "to be agreeable"—which leads me to ask, have you noticed this tall poppy syndrome playing out before us on social media, not just in Australia, but around the world? Even beyond social media, if you were to walk onto the campus of a majority of American universities, for example, holding a Bible, I can guarantee you within seconds you would feel immense pressure to "become agreeable" and hide it away.

The question is, will you personally bow to the pressure or not? Or will you stand alone? This prevalent desire to not rock the boat, stay low, to not stand up, and to stay away from anything that feels uncomfortable has consumed our world. Take note, this was the very thing Vashti did. She refused to come before the king because of the discomfort of his request. I assume she did not want to be ridiculed or looked on undesirably in front of the court officials. However, it was not this action alone that cost her the throne; rather, it was the threat that her actions could initiate—encouraging millions of women into rebellion.

Finally, the noun from her name *she* denotes a sheep or goat. This word appears to be like our word *head* as it describes a flock or herd. What speaks to me about this is a herd of other sheep following the head, almost unquestionably. This leads to a conversation between Memucan, one of the king's wise men who confronted the king saying:

> Queen Vashti has wronged not only the king, but all the officials and the peoples who are in every one of King Ahasuerus's provinces. For the queen's actions will become public knowledge to all the women and cause them to despise their husbands and say, "King Ahasuerus ordered Queen Vashti brought before him, but she did not come." Before this day is over, the noble women of Persia and Media who hear about the queen's act will say the same thing to all the king's officials, resulting in more contempt and fury (**Esther 1:16-18 CSB**).

Memucan recognized that Vashti was like the head of a herd, where women across their provinces would likely revolt in unison, following the head or lead of Vashti.

Before I divulge more about this topic, I ask you to hear me out. I am in no way suggesting that women should be mere commodities to men, or that our lives were designed to be nothing more than groveling servants to a man who only sees us as a trophy. I believe that God created women different in strength, unique in our qualities, but equal in value. God's design was for women to stand alongside their men, and together they would help one another.

In the perspective of Vashti's refusal, it could be viewed that her defiance was against a chauvinist-type king; yet in clearer view of her name and its meaning, we can see that this wasn't the case. Vashti's actions defied her role and responsibility. Her actions were divisive and would have sent out a "loud roar with destruction in mind" to her subjects across the kingdom. Had her motions been allowed to stand, it would have devastated, ruined, and weakened the kingdom, thus causing them to become vulnerable to surrounding enemies.

Upon some further study, I found that Greek translations of the text identify Vashti as Amestris. Some scholars believe that the mention of Amestris in varying translations is, in fact, Vashti. For if King Ahasuerus has been translated to Artaxerxes, and also Xerxes, it is highly likely that Vashti too, had a different translation of her name. I stumbled upon many a commentary, almost unanimously agreeing that Amestresis is Vashti. If this is indeed the case, then what does Amestris mean? The name is of Old Persian descent, and incredibly, it is a variation of the name Esther. This has brought scholars some confusion as they believe it to be Esther's name, but in the context of verses, the name Amestris in Greek translations is only described in relation to the verses mentioning Vashti. So with that in mind, it means "strong woman" and "Ishtar is my mother."[1] What and who, then, is Ishtar? And what is the significance of her being Vashti's mother?

Ishtar, was known as a goddess in the ancient world, and I'll be speaking of her throughout this book and teaching you in more depth about her later on. She is not some mystical spirit reserved just for the ancient world, but an ever-present demonic principality in our day today. She just looks different from that of a goddess sitting atop a temple. Yet if you look closely, you'll see her workings everywhere.

Paying attention to what Memucan said about Vashti's actions, we understand just what was at stake. God has anointed women like watchwomen on the walls, we have been gifted to see beyond the horizon where an incoming enemy is on the approach. Vashti however, revealed an opposite spirit to a watchman on the wall— she chose selfish defiance, she stood to tear down the safety of families and provinces that stretched far and wide.

Memucan's words to the king ring loud and true to our day, *"her actions will cause women to despise their husbands."* Memucan's name means "certain and true." He was speaking certain truth, recognizing the severity of the queen's actions and the fallout that would soon ensue if they did not address this betrayal swiftly. In short, Vashti's name in Arabic means "beautiful one." To a Hebrew audience, her name meant "when drinking." Scholars agree, her name collectively means "beautiful, when drinking." Then, when partnered with her Persian name of "daughter of Ishtar," we quickly understand that Vashti was the servant of a demonic principality.

This same principality is operating in our day today; she is considered beautiful and lovely. Amestris can also translate to mean "friend." Daughters of today's generations are listening to Ishtar and Vashti collectively, as though they are warm and gentle friends. They have become enamored and drunk on her seduction. She has captured the hearts of millions of young men and women, boys and girls, convincing them of her artful and deceitful lies. It is the very thing Memucan feared and warned would happen.

Women everywhere have grown to despise men; and many young men as a result, have taken on forms of femininity they were never designed to be. Breaking down the family unit, Ishtar has cunningly chipped away at the fabrics of God's articulate plan, bit by bit, destroying the sanctity of the womb, and introducing every demon-inspired ideology that goes against God's design. The result? The nations have been weakened, just as Memucan foretold.

It is profound then that it was Memucan—certain and true—who righted this wrong. By speaking the certain truth and not bowing to any pressure to please the king, he removed the daughter queen of Ishtar. I am sure he likely felt trepidation speaking of the removal of Vashti, yet his boldness paved way for the fall of this queen of hearts and for the rise of the true queen of God's heart, Esther. Could it be that the Lord is looking to dethrone this principality in our day, in order that Esther would arise as the true antidote for these demon strongholds that have become graves in the throats of countless women?

I believe the Lord is looking for wise men and women, who, like Memucan, will stand in the certain truth of God's infallible Word and refuse to move, calling out in the public square, irrespective of the intimidation to stay on a level playing field, and instead will shout, "Vashti must fall, depose the daughter of Ishtar, remove this false queen of hearts!" I prophesy the Lord is raising up such men and women who will stand in the courts of the King and cry out this certain truth that "these principalities and ideologies must be torn down."

ROAR, ESTHER, ROAR

In October 2020, I stood on the Washington Mall alongside thousands of other believers as we prayed on the eve of Amy Coney Barrett's Supreme Court Justice appointment. If you've followed me for any amount of time or read any of my previous books, you'll know how important this night was. That evening was one of the most profound in my life, most significantly because it was a confirmation to me of the mantle of Esther that God was beginning to pour out upon the earth.

As I wrote in Chapter 1, God had been highlighting the numbers 414 for an entire year leading up to this day. In fact, all year long I could not shake this message. In September of that year, through a moment of encounter with the Holy Spirit, I had written and recorded a spoken prophetic word that I released at the beginning of October 2020, and I called that word, "The mantle of Esther." In awe, I watched as multitudes of comments streamed in, almost collectively saying, "I have been seeing 414 everywhere. I didn't know what this meant until now."

I have noticed that God loves to orchestrate a tapestry of the same message all the way across the body of Christ around the world. It was a beautiful moment for I realized I was not alone, there were countless other women to whom the Lord was trumpeting this message. I'm sure, with this book in your hands, you are among those He has been speaking to about Esther.

As we stood with mud-soaked feet in the frigid cold on the Washington Mall that rainy October afternoon, a man by the name of Lou Engle (whom we now call friend and, affectionately, Papa Lou) took the stage as the crowd prayed. We had not known Lou personally before this night, but as these words began to pour out of his mouth, I listened in awe. Lou shared a dream that he had. These are the words he spoke:

In a dream, I was in a place, it was an open field with red rocks behind it. As far and wide as I could see, I saw women, young girls, teenagers, mothers, women coming from everywhere it was like a revival, a buzz. In the dream, I am the only man there with my intercessor friend, and he gives me his old Bible. I now understand that the old Bible represents an ancient calling, the ancient calling of Mordecai to mobilize the Esthers because these women were coming from everywhere. They were coming to hear the book of Esther be taught. A woman then stood up and she was teaching the book of Esther, and she said, "And these two words in the book of Esther actually mean, 'NAZGUL.'" I exploded out of the dream knowing exactly what it meant. It's from the third part of the movie, the *Lord of the Rings,* where the Nazgul witch king is destroying the armies of men and he said, "There is no man that can kill me," but the king's daughter takes off her helmet, let's down her hair and looks at the Nazgul and declares, "I am no man!" With that, she pierces the witch king. I realized the Lord was speaking, "I am going to raise up an Esther movement that will have the authority over witchcraft, authority over the death culture and the ideologies that are rising. God has always used women throughout the Bible to counteract the enemies' plans."[2]

Standing in the crowd, my jaw dropped, almost hitting the ground in absolute astonishment. Unbeknown to Lou or anyone but Nate on the Mall that day, I had had a dream earlier that same month that spoke into the dream that Lou had just shared from the stage. It was not lost on me that these two dreams collided on the very Mall where Martin Luther King Jr. declared, "I have a dream." I had just met Lou and his beautiful wife, Therese, only moments before he took the stage. He had heard of the prophetic word I had released about Esther and sought me out to ask about it. This was indeed a *kairos* moment. I share with you this very dream from my journal writings from earlier that morning:

October 12, 2020

I dreamt last night that I was in Washington, DC. In the dream, I saw myself standing on a large stage that was on the Washington Mall, we were facing the Washington Monument with our backs to the Capitol behind us. Before me was a sea of women, as far as the eye could see, at least a million of them and they were in travail.

On the stage, Lou Engle stood beside me. Lou was holding a microphone in the dream, and he was rocking back and forth under the anointing, he was standing to my right, and then he suddenly turned to me and, handing me the microphone he shouted, "Prophesy, Christy!"

Right then, a woman appeared to my left, I recognized her as someone from my past, but she transformed into Ursula, the sea-witch from the *Little Mermaid*. Her tentacles were all up on the stage, and there was ink from them leaking onto the floor. She was intimidating, and she viciously grabbed the microphone out of my hands, I shrunk back and took a step backward. She began to laugh. Lou then turned to me and asked in alarm, "What are you doing? Get the microphone off her!" As he said that, I suddenly felt a rumbling in the pit of my stomach, almost like a hungry, angry growl. Something about that gave me courage and I leapt forward and wrestled the microphone out of her hands. At that moment, a lion's roar burst up out of my spirit and through the microphone, this sound roared out over the sea of women.

It's almost as if I could physically see the roar like a sound wave—it hit the entire crowd, from the front all the way to the back. As it did, it stirred up a roar within each woman, and they then roared back. The sound of their collective roar burst into the atmosphere and like a sonic boom, was sent back like a wave to us on the stage. It hit Lou and I with a mighty force causing us to fall back under the weight of it (I noticed at that point Ursula disappeared). We watched as the roar traveled to the Supreme Court building behind us and hit it with power. I then saw a gargoyle that was sitting at the very top (in a crouched position) fall to the ground and it smashed into a million pieces. That was the end.

The following is the interpretation I had written:

I believe there is a significant moment coming when perhaps God is going to call a sea of women to pray and contend over America (Washington DC signifying the heart of the nation). This didn't feel like just any dream I've had before, this felt profound and REAL as though I was standing there. I'm not certain if this is speaking into an actual gathering of women or the calling of a sea of women to pray. It's interesting it was on the Mall, where great movements have taken place in the past. I'm reminded specifically of Martin Luther King Jr. who proclaimed there, "I have a dream." Perhaps, this is the dream of God for this hour. Women praying in travail to turn the tide of history. Esthers confronting the principalities of today.

Lou Engle represents these very movements; he is like an Elijah, ushering in the voice of the Lord. And interestingly in the dream, I believe he represented Elijah. When Ursula appeared beside me (I knew her to represent Jezebel), Lou turned to me and asked, "What are you doing? Take back the microphone." In other words, he was telling me, "Take back your voice."

Ursula appeared as the character from the movie, *The Little Mermaid*. I looked up what Ursula means and it is defined as "she-bear." I see her to be the counterfeit voice of feminism in modern-day women. She steals the voice of Ariel from the little mermaid. Ariel's name means "Lion of God." This is interesting because it was the roar of the lion of the Tribe of Judah that came up out of me, roared over the crowd, and it was the lion's roar that roared back through them.

What is intriguing is that Ursula first looked like this woman from my past (who was notorious for shutting down my voice. Her name means "white shadow"). I wonder if this speaks of people who appear to have the presence of Jesus (white) but ultimately have dark or insidious motives and intentions (shadow). I distinctly remember her tentacles on the stage with ink from them dripping all around. I remember thinking, *Ew!* in the dream. I believe this speaks of the caution of the Lord to not allow compromise (the ink) of Jezebel in the presence of God's holiness (the stage or the place where His Word was going forth).

It also stands out to me that Lou triggered the roar inside me, which I believe speaks to his anointing as a father and a Mordecai-type figure. Ultimately, it was his standing for righteousness (when he refused to partner with Jezebel on the stage) that was the very thing that triggered my roar as well as the roar of the sea of women. I believe God has positioned him for this calling in this hour. When the roar from the multitude hit the Supreme Court, I know more than I know, that this was the stronghold of Roe v Wade falling, and possibly even pointing to the stronghold of feminism that will fall in the days to come.

In hindsight, and with what I now know about the principality of Ishtar, I believe where I wrote about the stronghold of feminism, it was indeed the principality of Ishtar falling from a high place of governance. I want to add to my interpretation about the gargoyle. I recently looked up what gargoyles represent, and why, of all places, we see them atop ancient gothic churches and government buildings, like the one in my dream that sat atop the Greek architecture of the Supreme Court.

I discovered that gargoyles date back to ancient Greece and Egypt. They were originally designed as downspouts, to direct rainwater away from infrastructure, and therefore, their name comes from the French word *gargouille,* which means "throat." Their purpose, however, was twofold. They were also believed to redirect evil spirits, kind of odd considering how evil they themselves look, but this description is what was eye-opening to me—"they are designed to protect what they guard." Why would God show me a gargoyle atop the Supreme Court building? He was revealing the demonic principality that was guarding its territory over legislation in the United States. When you consider how volatile things have become regarding righteous legislation, I am prompted by this verse from Romans 3:13 (ESVUK): *"Their **throat** is an open grave; they use their tongues to deceive." "The venom of asps is under their lips."*

If you take a closer look at the topic of abortion, for example, you will notice how the tongue has been used to deceive countless women into believing that the slaughter of their own children is for their empowerment—the throat is an open grave. "My body, my choice." In truth, the body of the child is not the body of the mothers, and no one has the right or choice to murder another human being. Yet, this principality has deceived millions, not just through abortion, but as I will show you, through the witchcraft ideology of modern-day feminism and the messaging of the feminist empowerment movement in our day.

I believe the gargoyle in my dream represents both abortion and feminism—or more aptly, Ishtar. Jezebel too is a mere servant of this higher principality of Ishtar. They go hand in hand, and I will reveal to you how God is raising up an army of women, cloaked in the mantle of Esther, to counteract the deceitful tongue of this enemy principality that has led millions of babies and mothers into the throat of its grave, among a myriad of other insidious ideologies.

It's time for Vashti and her mother goddess, Ishtar, to fall.

NOTES

1. Amestris, *Behind the Name;* https://www.behindthename.com/ name/amestris/submitted; accessed April 10, 2024.

2. Lou Engle message transcribed from Let Us Worship, YouTube; https://youtu.be/i3p8oPrn-Cg?si=V1p8yQxMwavt3jiB; accessed May 22, 2024.

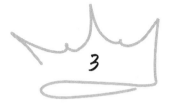

YOUR CORONATION

BIBLE READING: ESTHER 2:1-10

Have you ever pondered Esther's upbringing? I mean, truly examined her life? I felt the Holy Spirit impressing me to really consider what it means to carry her mantle—not just the aspects of bravery and courageousness, but the hard and difficult parts of her calling too. Her orphanhood, the fact she was an exile, and living in a foreign country with an adoptive father. The hard truth that she was whisked away, likely around the age of 14-16, from all that she had known, to sleep with a foreign king.

As a Jew, this would have been a defilement against herself and her heritage. It's important we look at all the details of her life, not just the parts we find admirable. For I believe that if we are to carry this mantle of Esther with integrity and triumph, we must also take the matters of our hearts before the Lord. Esther was required to go through a time of purification, and what if the Lord is requiring this of you and me as well? There is a saying in ministry that your gift can only carry you as far as your character will allow. The same rings true for this mantle. If you attempt to carry Esther's mantle, exposing and tearing down principalities of today without allowing the Holy Spirit to enter in and heal wounds of the heart, the mantle will crush you.

HEALING THE ORPHAN HEART

"You will have a hard life, one marked with disappointment and sadness, but God will use it for His glory." Those were the harsh words spoken over my life by a guest prophet at a church I was visiting one Sunday morning. For reference, I use the terms *prophet* and *prophetic* very loosely when retelling this story.

I was just ten years old and visiting a church other than my own that morning with my friend and her family on a Sunday playdate. My friend and I had been happily enjoying ourselves in the Sunday school class when someone rushed in and called all the children to go to the main auditorium because the guest wanted to prophesy over us. I vividly remember hearing the prophetic words he delivered over other children before he got to me, those words were filled with hope and expectation. I waited nervously to hear what he might say over my life.

As a shy and introverted ten-year-old, my nerves were having a field day inside me. I hated any limelight or extreme attention, and the mere thought of someone speaking over me on a microphone while the entire congregation looked on was causing inner panic. Yet it was my anticipation that he was going to say something amazing as he was saying over the other children. So rather than run away, as I desperately wanted to do, I remained. What is more, I had no understanding of the prophetic. Even though I was familiar with prayer lines, I had no idea what prophecy was and what was happening in that moment. I do remember one thing though, a hunger for this speaker to approve of me, to say something good about me and my future. Something inside me was longing to hear what God had to say, at least what I thought was God speaking.

With about 20 children before me, this man's feet finally landed in front of mine, and waiting nervously I looked up at him. He stood back and paused for a moment before abruptly delivering these words, "You will have a hard life, one marked with disappointment and sadness, but God will use it for His glory." I still remember the manner in which he delivered this "prophecy." The first sentence was spoken slowly, drawn out and pensive, then, "but God will use it for His glory" kind of fell out of his mouth like a rushed afterthought.

He then boorishly lay his hand upon my head as though he were branding my soul with a hot searing iron to seal what had been spoken before promptly moving on to the next child to my right. I recall the overwhelming sensation of utter humiliation washing over me, I had never felt humiliation with such force before, followed quickly by waves of rejection as I listened to the word he gave directly after mine. My friend happened to be the child standing to my right, and she was naturally beautiful to behold. Not to devalue myself in any way, but even as a young girl this friend had a rare and effortless beauty about her. To be honest though, I'd never even questioned any contrast between my friend and I until this very moment.

As the speaker moved past me and stood before her, he began to proclaim how beautiful she was, even creating a spectacle by having her turn around and face the congregation behind her as he said, "You are just like Queen Esther, beautiful to look upon. God has given you the anointing of Esther and you will save a nation just as she did." Those words also branded into my memory, like a freshly scorched wound, just as deeply as the words spoken over my life.

I remember wanting to run out of the room at that moment, to hide in a corner and cry. Was I not as worthy of a word like that because I was apparently not as beautiful as she? That day was the beginning of a root of insecurity that began to imbed itself deeply into my heart for years to come. I'll share later in Chapter 6 about these roots and how the Holy Spirit brought them to the surface and healed them; but for now, I highlight this moment for a reason.

I also want to emphasize, this is not to say that the word over my friend was inaccurate, but merely to draw attention to the fact that true prophecy is not based on looks alone. God looks at the heart. True prophecy also does not deliver a word that incites fear or humiliation. If it was a warning word, God always releases hope and answers with a warning. Yet I never felt that the latter part of this "prophecy," where he said, "but God will use it for His glory" was a true depiction of hope and solution. It felt unfair—why would a good and kind God lead me through a hard life just to use it for His own glory?

As a child, that moment also elicited an unhealthy fear of God— He suddenly seemed mean and unfeeling. From that day forward, I could never read the book of Esther without a sting pricking at my heart. So for many years, even into my adulthood, I avoided reading this book in the Bible. I felt unworthy, uncalled, unqualified, and even jealous that God would supposedly give me something harsh, while giving others something beautiful. I share this story with you because I believe many daughters have disqualified themselves from the mantle and anointing of Esther, for one reason or another. Maybe like me, you have received a "prophetic word" (using that term loosely again) from a pastor or a friend, a word that incited insecurity rather than hope and purpose.

Could it be, daughter, that you have had similar lies spoken over you? Perhaps untrue words spoken by loved ones or someone in leadership in your life? A parent or family member, spouse, pastor, teacher, or someone you looked up to? They may have been words of judgment, accusation, or even mockery that made you question your worth and value? Words that made you question your calling and even your beauty. Words that branded your identity illegitimately and have marked you for months, perhaps years? Have you disqualified yourself because of those words or thoughts in your mind? Have you considered yourself not as beautiful as Esther is described and therefore dismissed your name from Esther's mantle because you feel you can't relate? Have you discounted yourself because you don't feel as courageous or as brave as her? Have you felt yourself unworthy? Have you considered yourself a nobody?

Maybe you picked up this book out of mere curiosity, or maybe it's because something deep down inside you says, "Dig a little deeper past the lies." I pray the following words you read in this book, would fall like water upon the dry and parched soil of your heart. I pray that these words, inspired by the Holy Spirit, would rebrand you with the anointing and mantle of Esther that you are truly called to.

I want you to read these following words that are not from me, but from the Father Himself:

This is who you are, My daughter. You are a daughter of the Most High God, set apart for this moment of time, specifically for the purposes to which I have called you. This is your crowning, My daughter, out from hiding and into calling. You are not an afterthought; and though your life may have been marked by pain, I never caused the pain—though I will now use it to turn it back upon the head of the enemy. Allow Me to reset the foundations of truth in the depths of your soul. Pain and circumstance do not determine your destiny. Your identity *is* My daughter, a daughter of the King, this is who you are. I see you as beautiful; why would you ever compare the unique beauty of who you are to another? I made you uniquely, and your uniqueness is exquisite. I break the lies of the enemy over your heart, mind, and identity, for I am leading you into complete healing in this hour. I need you healed and whole so I can release this mantle of Esther upon you, to a world that is broken and in need of your testimony. Are you willing, My daughter? I am calling you forth, for such a time as this.

EXILE OF HEART

Upon studying the book of Esther, I have come to conclude, based on Esther's childhood, that she too must have wrestled with doubts and insecurities. I imagine that she would have tangled with thoughts of inferiority and unworthiness. How, you may ask? After all, she was a queen, she had everything she could ever need, and she was beautiful beyond compare. To answer that question, allow me to show you some details of her life that are all too often overlooked. For context, let's re-read Esther 2:5-7 (CSB):

> *In the fortress of Susa, there was a Jewish man named Mordecai son of Jair, son of Shimei, son of Kish, a Benjaminite. Kish had been taken into exile from Jerusalem with the other captives when King Nebuchadnezzar of Babylon took King Jeconiah of Judah into exile. Mordecai was the legal guardian of his cousin, Hadassah (that is, Esther), because she had no father or mother. The young woman had a beautiful figure and was extremely good looking. When her father and mother died, Mordecai had adopted her as his own daughter.*

Very little is mentioned about Esther's childhood, aside from these verses and a few other tiny details mentioned throughout her book; but there are two significant details that stand out to me in these three verses alone.

The first being, Mordecai, Esther's adoptive uncle (or cousin), was taken into exile from Jerusalem, which means Esther, too, was an exile. If we stop and pause on this piece of information for a moment, and really take into consideration what that must have been like for her, you gain a broader appreciation for what she does later in her story. Though Scripture does not tell us where she was born, whether in Israel or in Persia, there is no mistaking, Esther was an outsider, a political refugee from her homeland of Israel. A captive of political upheaval.

Very few people understand what it's like to move from one country to another, and all the discomforts associated with that. Nate and I moved internationally from Australia to the United States in 2023, and though the two countries have similar Western values and comforts, the differences between these two nations are polarizing when you have lived in both.

We constantly live in a state of two worlds, missing parts of one, while loving the parts of the other. I once read, "If you continually look back and compare your home country to the new country you are living in, you will never learn to appreciate and enjoy all that your new home has to offer…." That advice has always stuck with me, and I wonder if Esther had to adapt and do the same.

I had to learn to separate the two nations in my heart, or I would be in a constant state of comparison, which as the saying goes, "Comparison is the thief of joy." There were little things I was so familiar with growing up that I didn't realize I'd miss until they were gone when we moved to a new land—and that's not necessarily a bad thing, it's just different. Details like the weather, for example. I miss the rainy season and storms during the summer as we lived in a tropical climate; but in our new hometown, we get the beauty of snow. I have had to learn to adapt in little ways I never anticipated.

Yet Nate and I moved of our own free will (and calling from God). Esther, on the other hand, was not so fortunate. Whether she had been born in exile or her exile took place after her birth, the fact remains that her family had been forcibly taken from their home. I can only imagine what that must have felt like for her and her fellow Jewish people now living in Persia. The constant feeling of loss, while having to remain and find new ways to live and thrive. Not to mention their worship of God, and their strict Jewish customs and laws. Simple things such as the way they washed and prepared their food were carried out in strict Jewish customs to avoid uncleanliness and the association with sin. Yet culturally, the Persians didn't believe in one God like the Jews; instead, they worshipped *auramazda,* a goddess, and their own selves, as later seen in Haman. Esther lived in a state of exile, and had to learn to adapt to this foreign nation of which she had no heritage.

Second, and perhaps a detail that is most significant to her childhood, is the fact that she was an orphan. Esther 2:7 mentions this detail twice: *"Mordecai was the legal guardian of his cousin Hadassah (that is, Esther), because she had no father or mother.... When her father and mother died, Mordecai had adopted her as his own daughter."* Before I dive into the orphan piece, I want to make mention that there is a beautiful illustration in this verse—where each time Esther's orphanhood is mentioned, Mordecai is also mentioned. He is her safeguard and protector, which tells us she was never alone. When Scripture mentions something twice, it's because God wants us to pay close attention to this detail.

In a similar manner to her exile, we don't know when Esther lost both her parents, or how this happened, yet we know it took place at some point in her childhood as we see that Mordecai assumed the role of her guardian and father. This leads me to wonder about Esther, how did the loss of her parents impact her as a child? Did it instill fear within her that is not usual of a girl her age? Or was she too young to remember? Did it alter her views and perceptions of God? You see, every detail in Scripture is written with purpose, and this aspect of Esther's orphanhood is no different. Was she old enough to remember her parents? These are all worthy questions to ask, because losing a parent is traumatic, no matter how young or old, let alone losing both during childhood. Which leads me to believe that she would have surely battled with some of the characteristics of an orphan.

Though every child deals with trauma in different and unique ways, I feel it is important for us to look at these characteristics that can often play out in our own hearts—situations that have happened along this path of life that may have left us brokenhearted or worse, feeling abandoned and alone. Facing past circumstances is crucial to address, because as we see with Esther, she went through a time of preparation before her appointed time of destiny. Many of us want the crowns, we want the mantle and anointing without first dealing with the issues of our hearts and character. I'm not writing this to condemn you, but because it is on the heart of God to see His daughters completely freed; otherwise, this mantle will crush you.

When the Holy Spirit began leading me through my own healing of heart and mind, I began to recognize the ways I had viewed God and life through the eyes of an orphan. He would bring to my remembrance memories such as the one I shared with you at the beginning of this chapter, and He would lead me into Truth over the lies I had believed. When He led me to this memory, I recall weeping over it, as He first instructed me to forgive the man who prophesied the lie. Then, God showered me in the truth saying, "Daughter, I have called you to carry the mantle of Esther." What's more, in writing this book, the lie that the enemy intended upon my life to silence me has backfired against him.

Many Christians today give their lives to Jesus, but never follow through with the renewal of their minds. Romans 12:2 (ESVUK) instructs us, *"Do not be conformed to this world, but be transformed by the renewal of your mind, that by testing you may discern what is the will of God, what is good and acceptable and perfect."* When true testing comes, they buckle under the weight of past experiences, lies they have believed and the fear of man. The word Paul used for *renewing* of the mind, is the Greek word, *anakainόsis*[1] and it means *aná*, "up, completing a process," which intensifies *kainō,* "make fresh, new, new development; a renewal, achieved by God's power." Christian doctors have discovered that reading the Word of God and applying it to our lives creates complete and new, neural pathways in our mind. In other words, God rewrites our history, our memories and emotions, through discovering what *He* has to say about us.

As one such example, when God led the Israelites out of Egypt, His plan was to lead them to their Promised Land, a mere 40-day journey. Yet Egypt never left their minds, and they resisted the renewal. God knew even then that the battles lying in wait for them to possess their Promised Land would have killed them with their slavery-orphan mindset that they refused to address. Instead, they continued to complain and moan.

Rather than celebrate the fact that God had delivered them in a powerful way, they even pined for their life of slavery back in Egypt, for it was familiar to them. It's intriguing that one of the definitions of the word *renewal* in Romans 12:2 is "completing a process which intensifies." It's not a comfortable process to surrender our past to God; but if we don't, let the Israelites who died in the wilderness serve as a reminder that the pain of our past is not worth holding on to. An entire generation, including Moses, never entered the Promised Land. You and I must shed our hearts of the orphan and slavery mindset to move forward in the mantle of Esther. If we don't, we will crumble at the moment of adversity and testing. When our courage is needed, we will not be able to step into it.

I want you to seriously reflect upon these definitions of an orphan mentality, and ask the Holy Spirit to highlight any traits in which you have been unknowingly (or even knowingly) operating.

Characteristics of an orphan:

- The constant feeling of being overlooked. You often say to yourself, "No one sees me or notices me. I'm not important or well-known enough. I don't have what it takes." Or, "No matter what I do, it's never enough."

- You act in rejection or you reject yourself before others get a chance to reject you. You struggle to hold on to friendships or relationships because of this.

- You have a constant fear of abandonment, always worried about being left alone or in fear of a spouse or friend cheating on you. (Possibly rooted in a spouse cheating or an unfaithful father or mother.)

- You hoard comforts. This doesn't necessarily mean you hoard trash; rather, it can seem as if you don't want to step out of your comfort zone, ever. You like to always feel comfortable.

- You desire to be wholly independent, not dependent on any man or even a family member. You feel safest in your control only.

- You have a desperation to prove your worth to others, always boasting to everyone about your achievements, and working constantly to let people know that you are not a failure.

- You have an insatiable desire to be noticed and celebrated.

I wonder, in reflection, can you see any of those characteristics revealing themselves within your own character? Do you perceive God through the eyes of fear and abandonment? I know I did. Do you find yourself rejecting yourself before others can reject you? I know I used to. Do you struggle with relationships or submitting to authority in your life? I certainly did. Or perhaps there are more subtle characteristics such as feeling afraid at the thought of giving your heart completely and wholly to the Lord. Do you desire to be independent from Him because you fear His rejection? Yet again, this was true of me. The characteristics of an orphan can manifest in many ways and the root of which can be more subtle than you may realize.

If any of those traits sound familiar to how you perceive life, I want you to prayerfully walk through with the following three actions:

1. Put down this book and ask the Holy Spirit to show you where the root started. He may bring to your memory a moment of deep pain or rejection. Don't run from

it—ask Him to lead you into healing through it, and remember He is holding your hand. You are not alone.

2. Then forgive those who need to be forgiven. This may be the most painful part to let go of; if you struggle with that, just picture yourself giving that person (or persons) to Jesus in forgiveness.

3. Now, *renew* your mind. Ask the Holy Spirit to show you *His truth* over that situation and the lies that were spoken over you. Then, open your Bible. A verse may come to your mind or you may be led to a verse, but you will know that it's His truth because it will speak hope directly to that point of pain. Wait until you get the word from Him, and I promise, the truth will reveal and heal.

ESTHER'S TIME OF PURIFICATION

Esther was required to go through a season of purification before stepping into her role as queen. Could our own purification involve the process of allowing the Holy Spirit to heal parts of our hearts that have been broken and hurt from past seasons? This is a step that cannot be missed if we are to fully carry the cloak of her mantle for the days ahead. If we don't go through this purification, we will find ourselves unable to discern the voice of God in the moment when we need it the most. In Esther 2:8-9 (BSB) we read:

When the king's command and edict had been pro-
claimed, many young women gathered at the citadel
of Susa under the care of Hegai. Esther was also taken
to the palace and placed under the care of Hegai,
the custodian of the women. And the young woman
pleased him and obtained his favor, so he quickly pro-
vided her with beauty treatments and the special diet.
He assigned to her seven select maidservants from the
palace and transferred her with them to the best place
in the harem.

I want to highlight Hegai to you, for I believe he is the picture of the Holy Spirit in Esther's story. Amazingly, the Persian meaning of *Hegai* means "Meditation, word, groaning, separation." His characteristics are synonymous with the Holy Spirit. Romans 8:26 (NIV) tells us that *"the Spirit helps us in our weakness. We do not know what we ought to pray for, but the Spirit himself intercedes for us through wordless groans."* Too few have a relationship with Him; and I believe that to carry this mantle of Esther in the days to come will require the help of the Holy Spirit. Are you acquainted with Him, daughter? He is your greatest Helper in this hour, your strength, support, and guard. What I find most beautiful about this part of Esther's story is that Hegai steps in to protect her, where Mordecai physically cannot. The word *custodian* is *shamar*[2] and means "a bodyguard, to attend to, careful to keep, defender, gate-keeper, watchman and sentry." Hegai is an exquisite depiction of the Holy Spirit.

We often look at eunuchs in ancient history as something abhorrent, something bizarre, something strange. They were known to be castrated, though not all were. What then, is their relevance in this story, as they are mentioned on several occasions. Personally, I believe where it pertains to Hegai in particular, it is speaking of being set apart unto the voice of the Holy Spirit alone.

Esther had a close relationship with Hegai, but it wasn't sexual, yet, it was intimate. This too speaks of our relationship with the Holy Spirit, who is our Guard and Protector. I fear too many daughters have not become acquainted with the Watchman of their hearts, and now is the time. For He is the One who will instruct you in the days to come, of what you need to do. Hegai was the one who advised Esther what to take into the room with her, when it was her time to go to the king. Likewise, the Holy Spirit is the One who leads us in all wisdom—we cannot carry this mantle without Him. Do you have a relationship with Him? If not, ask Him to come close, invite the Spirit of God to teach and instruct you, that you may hear Him, just as Esther heeded Hegai.

OIL OF MYRRH

Esther 2:12 (ESVUK) says:

> Now when the turn came for each young woman to go in to King Ahasuerus, after being twelve months under the regulations for the women, since this was the regular period of their beautifying, six months with oil of myrrh and six months with spices and ointments for women.

The oil of myrrh was used as part of Esther's beauty treatments and purification, and it might sound familiar to you in relation to Jesus. Myrrh had two main purposes: anointing and embalming. Myrrh was first mentioned in Scripture as a principal ingredient in the holy anointing oil. It speaks to us today of our own death and resurrection in Christ Jesus. Myrrh is prophetic of letting go of the old you and stepping into the anointing of who you really are as a daughter of the king.

I wonder, was Esther required to receive six months of beautifying with the oil of myrrh, as it represented the complete death of her old life and everything she had dreamed? I certainly can testify, I've been there. I know what it is to let go of something that I thought was a dream for my life—the place I loved to live, for example. It's possible, daughter, that the Lord will lead you through seasons of myrrh as well—a time of surrender, letting go of what you thought would be, and giving yourself to Him, no matter the cost. It sounds more romantic than it feels. The death of the old, so that the birth of the new can come.

Observe how myrrh was used for both burial and anointing. You might recall that the wise men who brought gifts for Jesus laid before Him gold, frankincense, and myrrh. This wasn't just some happenstance. They didn't bring Him three precious gifts just so we could one day sing carols with fanciful words, no. Myrrh was brought as a prophetic symbol—a declaration that this was the anointed King who was born to die, to endure death upon a Cross, so we could live.

Myrrh points to the body and Blood of Jesus. When Jesus was upon the Cross, this oil was brought before Him once again; this time, offered mixed with wine. *"And they gave him to drink wine mingled with myrrh: but he received it not"* (Mark 15:23 KJV). When myrrh was mixed with wine, it became a sedative of sorts. Jesus refused because He knew He had to endure the full wrath of the Cross—He had to die, so we may live. *Myrrh* means "bitter." Jesus instead drank the bitter cup of our sins, and carried them for us, and we become beautified by receiving of His finished work.

The myrrh tree, from which the oil of myrrh is withdrawn, is a little scrub of a tree that grows alone in the desert. Inside the tree's bark it is red, like blood, and the exterior is white. This little tree announces the finished work of the Cross, the Blood poured out on our behalf that washes us clean—white as snow.

I believe that Esther's requirement for receiving myrrh as a beauty treatment speaks prophetically into receiving the beauty of the Cross. While yes, the cross was yet to occur in the natural, everything in scripture is a prophetic allegory that points to it. Esther's receiving of myrrh during her time of beautification is one such picture. A transformation takes place when we receive His broken body that He purposely and distinctly gave up for us. He gave us the gift of His life so we can walk in abundant life (John 10:10). The process of walking with the Holy Spirit leads us into the beauty of the Cross. Where we leave our old selves behind, and pick up His perfect completion instead. From this finished work, we carry the mantle of Esther in our day. Could this be what the purification of Esther represents? A complete transfer from the old into the new? I believe so, for it is here where she is ready to go to the king.

While we don't know all the details surrounding Esther's early childhood, where or when she lost her father and mother, or how she came to be in the foreign country of Persia, we know that

God brought her through a time of healing. Purification. Always remember that every detail in Scripture is written with purpose, and this information of Esther's orphanhood is no different.

Daughter, the Holy Spirit wants to take your hand in this season and lead you to the foot of the Cross, to behold the beauty of Jesus precious body hanging upon that old, rugged tree, so you can receive from Him. It's time to exchange your pain for His wholeness.

Daughter, I hear the Father calling, "Will you walk through this time of beautification with Me and trade your bitterness (the myrrh) for My love and affection for you? Take My hand, for I am your Guard and Gatekeeper, walk with the Holy Spirit and allow Him to lead you through purification. Behold Jesus, and you will come out beautified, looking just like Him. No more insecurities, daughter, for you are Mine, a daughter of the King. It's time to walk in the fullness of this calling."

NOTES

1. Strong's Greek Concordance #342.

2. Strong's Greek Concordance #8104.

PART TWO

the
ESTHER
Crowning

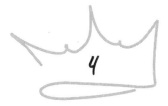

4

THE COST OF THE CALL

BIBLE READING: ESTHER 2:11-14

The year was 2011, and I woke up in the middle of the night in a sweat—something was happening to me that I was wholly unfamiliar with. *Am I unwell? Why do I feel this all-consuming grief and sorrow?* Gruesome visions of what I had read in a book the day before came flooding back to my mind and, as best as I can explain, a sound came out of the pit of my stomach that I had never heard before. It was an unstoppable force consuming me from the inside out, resulting in an uncontrollable howl that was bursting out of my mouth.

As I was yet to have children, I was unaware at the time, but in hindsight I sounded like a mother in childbirth. It shocked me and I felt embarrassed. Even though my husband, Nate, was asleep, I remember feeling desperately humiliated. "What's happening to me?" I remember crying out that question to God in anguish. It was 3 o'clock in the morning and I couldn't stop these urges, so I ran out of our bedroom to a room at the other end of the house and shut the door behind me.

I didn't want to wake Nate, but more than that I was so embarrassed that I didn't want him to hear me making these horrifying sounds of labor that I couldn't control. I remember looking heavenward as I sat on the floor on my knees, "What's wrong with me?" The Father's answer returned to me, "Nothing is wrong with you, you are being called."

Suddenly, the nightmarish images came to my mind once more and the wail returned. "What are You calling me to?" I cried out to the Lord. "You are in lament and travail, for I am calling you to pray to see the end of abortion." I then saw an image of myself worshipping to the lyrics of a song at a women's conference years earlier, where I was singing, "Break my heart for what breaks Yours." Only now did I realize the gravity of the request within those words. What I was feeling in this moment were the depths of God's heartbreak, He was allowing me to feel a measure of what He feels. I cannot overemphasize that it was beyond painful. I felt like my entire body was being torn in two. The travail continued all night long until the morning broke, and suddenly the lament stopped. I was finally able to fall back asleep for an hour or two.

The images I kept seeing throughout that night were painted in my mind through the words of a book that I had purchased at our local Christian bookstore just days earlier. The book was titled, *Unplanned* by Abby Johnson. I must warn you, what I am about to write, though brief in description, is difficult to read. To the dear mamas who have undergone an abortion, I ask you to pray before reading, I share these details because I believe the Lord no longer wants these horrors hidden in darkness. He wants it exposed to the light in order that He can heal. He longs to heal His daughters who have been deceived by the enemy to walk into the path of an abortion, and He longs to heal the coming generations from this grave injustice.

I wholeheartedly understand that it can be triggering and traumatizing for those who have been led by the lies of the enemy down this path. I want you to know that I don't condemn you, only the enemy condemns. The Greek word for *condemnation* is *katakrino* and it means "to hold one down." I believe the Lord wants to break the bonds of condemnation over any daughter reading this, who has been held down by this sin. I want to take a moment to pause and pray over those who have had abortions—will you pray with me? If that is you, daughter, I want you to read the following words and allow the Holy Spirit to wash the cleansing Blood of Jesus over you.

> *"Father, I ask for Your daughter who has been held by the bonds of condemnation. Your beloved daughter stands before you, she is broken and in repentance, please heal her wounds. Father, heal her scars as only You can. Show her the destiny, purpose, and hope You have for her, despite this tragedy. Redeem what has been lost and show her the child (or children) in heaven who are now with You, and praying with You for her. In Jesus's name, amen."*

I want you to know God *can* redeem *all* your past, including abortion. He forgives and washes clean when you repent before Him. So I encourage you to lay it all down before Him. God is kind and gracious and His arms are wide and outspread to you, waiting for you to run into them.

Don't carry condemnation for one moment longer, give it to Him. I see you releasing your testimony of this in the days to come, of what you have been through and how the Father has healed you. Your testimony will be as a lifeline to other women who need healing, or to those considering abortion. Your words will release the *life* of Jesus over them and their little ones in the womb. I also want you to know that your baby is safe in the arms of Jesus in Heaven, and they have purpose there, to pray for you and intercede for your destiny.

With that said, please only read the next two paragraphs if the Holy Spirit gives you peace to do so, if not, move to the next paragraph beyond that.

> I had read only a chapter or two of *Unplanned,* when Abby Johnson described the scene of being forced to hold a sonogram wand over the pregnant womb of a mother as she underwent an abortion at the Planned Parenthood facility where she was a director. Having worked there for years, advocating relentlessly for abortion, this was the first time Abby was witnessing one in real time. She had pieced together the parts of babies in the POC rooms (products of conception, or, as the staff called it, "parts of children" room). Yet she had never witnessed the process, until now. The pregnant mother was about to undergo a first-term abortion, and as circumstances would have it, Abby was required this day to hold the sonogram wand for the abortionist as he prepared his tools for the unthinkable. She moved the wand over the mother's belly, who was squirming and visibly in turmoil.
>
> The abortionist harshly told her to be quiet as he fired up the suction equipment. Abby watched in

alarm on the screen as the 12-week-old baby wriggled around, kicking contentedly, unaware of his or her imminent fate. Her heart racing, eyes glued, as the suction tool of the abortionist entered the mother's womb and became visible on the screen, moving like a wolf in the night, into the safety of the womb. The tiny baby, perceiving the threat, jumped in alarm, pulling away in the fetal position in a defense to protect his or herself. The abortionist moved closer, and setting the tool in position next to the little one's leg, he turned on the suction. Abby watched on in horror as the sounds of the tool began to tear away the little one's leg, followed by the visible blood going through the tubes as she shakily held the wand in place and witnessed the baby wrestling and writhing, fighting for its life, all to no avail. Piece by piece, she watched in horror as the innocent child was gruesomely murdered before her eyes, until there was nothing left on the screen but an empty womb. Upon reading this, I threw the book down in horror and let out a cry of agony.[1]

WEIGHING THE COST

It was those written images that led to my travail that night. I had no idea God was mantling me in that moment with the call of Esther—to stand and speak for those who cannot speak for themselves. At the time though, I had little understanding of what this mantle would cost me. In hindsight, I would have preferred to have had some form of warning about the cost, not that it would have prevented me from continuing in this calling, but that it would have saved me a lot of heartache by simply understanding what was happening.

As I began speaking with friends and family, sharing with them what God had opened my eyes to regarding abortion, friends began to disassociate with me, completely ending all contact with me without giving reason or regard. For example, I was attending a mother's home group at the time, it was a social outing that I looked forward to once a week. I was a full-time stay-at-home mother, so this home group with other new mothers was like a refreshing lifeline in the throes of early motherhood. I loved being a mum, but having a little time to myself and meeting with fellow mums, worshipping together, and talking about life and Jesus was like pouring water on a parched land.

One night I shared with the group what had happened to me and what the Lord had shown me regarding abortion. I told them how I felt God was leading me to start speaking up more about it, and praying with His daughters who had undergone abortions, to see healing restored in them. I didn't anticipate their reactions—what I shared was not well received. I admit, however, that my newfound calling and passion may have been somewhat shocking to hear—it was as if it had come out of nowhere.

The following day I opened a text: "We're changing up the home groups and shuffling everyone around, you'll be moved to a different group starting next week." I was shattered. I knew it was because of what I had shared the night before. Not surprisingly, I was the only one who was "shuffled" around. Yet I could not shift from this mantle. I had to keep going.

The more I persisted, the more resistance I faced. Family thought I was crazy; in fact, one distant family member told me I was like a hot air balloon, floating too high with my ideas, and that she was like a BB gun shooting me to the ground. I told her, "This hot air balloon is flying too high, out of your range." The resistance I was facing was perplexing. These were Christians, how could they be completely disregarding these silent horrors taking place in our own backyards, allowing mothers to be led to the slaughter? What of the heartbreak these mothers faced following the abortion of their son or daughter? Were we just happier to keep all this pain hidden and covered, never to see the light of day? Their silence was deafening. What's worse, they were blatantly ignoring commands of Scripture, including Proverbs 31:8-9, among many others.

Speak up for those who cannot speak for themselves, for the rights of all who are destitute. Speak up and judge fairly; defend the rights of the poor and needy (**Proverbs 31:8-9 NIV**).

The more I spoke, the more trouble it caused, yet the more determined I became. I received private messages from leaders telling me to be quiet after I shared on my Facebook page—and word was spreading fast that I had gone crazy.

Then something wonderful began to happen. I began receiving private messages from women in unplanned pregnancies, in dire need of support and encouragement. I found that despite the resistance I was facing, women were responding, albeit secretly, to receive courage and help, as very few were speaking into this issue at the time, and offering support. I was able to walk alongside many women and help them with natural means and the ultimate decision to choose life for their precious little ones, despite their difficult circumstances. Several happened to be "pastors' daughters" who approached me on separate occasions. All of whom had become pregnant either out of wedlock or in affairs. Many of whom were from well-known families. All of them were being encouraged to get abortions by their fathers and or the church leadership.

One young woman was even given a check, paid for by the church, to "do away with the evidence." I'll never forget pleading with her for her baby's life, offering that I would take the baby and adopt him or her myself. She almost didn't go through with it, but the pressure from her pastor father and church leadership essentially pushed her to the doors of the abortion clinic that day.

For every little life lost, I went through periods of grief for them, it broke me. I remember crying out to the Lord one day, "This is too heavy, take this from me." In that moment, I saw Jesus in the Garden of Gethsemane crying out the same thing. Though His burden was far graver and heavier than mine, I knew then, this was the cross He had asked me to carry. We will each be asked something similar. The question is, will you take it?

Jesus renewed in me a fresh resolve that I had to keep speaking and praying. I soon realized, this issue was deeper than I ever thought; hidden in our own congregations, there were broken women sitting on pews, silenced by those around them. If it was this bad within the church, how much worse outside of it?

I grew to endure the loneliness as I continued to face fierce opposition from churches, leaders, and pastors alike—not to mention, the most difficult of all, family and friends. I share all of this with you not to shame the Body of Christ, or even anyone in particular, but to highlight this reality and the urgent need for you to step into the calling God has for you. I believe the call of Esther has more often than not been romanticized to be viewed as merely beautiful, wonderful, fun, and adventurous. Though there certainly is beauty to it, in a much broader understanding, Esther's is a calling of surrender and sacrifice.

I want to emphasize, however, your calling will look different from mine. You may be called to speak and bring answers to the issues of abortion, or you may not be called to this specific injustice to the same degree that I am. What is important to distinguish is, whatever your calling, it can be lonely to walk a path when no one else understands what you're doing. Everyone wants to be called an Esther, but very few count the cost of her calling.

I believe many who will read these words are going to feel freed. Perhaps you've been walking a path alone, wondering why, and trying to figure out what you did wrong, trying to understand why you don't fit in with the status quo. You feel separated, not because you feel better than everyone else, but because of the calling deep within. You've been questioning yourself, as I did, "Am I crazy? What's wrong with me?" I am here to tell you, daughter, nothing is wrong with you. You are being mantled with the anointing and calling of Esther.

FROM THE HAREM TO THE PALACE

Few realize the sacrifice it takes to lay down one's life for what God has called them to, for the mantle of Esther is not a comfortable path to walk. I know this may not sound very encouraging in the moment, but I would be doing you a disservice if I merely tickled your ears with a fairy tale. I write this book for you, daughter, as well as my own daughters. I pray this is a light that guides your path forward. I say these things not to instill fear, but to give you direction, for I believe that we have deemed stories like Esther's as a whimsical fairy tale and not considered the full gravity of her call.

We all desire the beauty in the ending of her story, without counting the cost of the difficult steps that led her there. I wonder how many have forsaken the call because they were blindsided when opposition came? They questioned the calling upon their lives and disregarded it because they didn't understand that with calling comes opposition. It's not all roses and tulips; it's sometimes the valley of shadows and loneliness.

However with that said, I encourage you with this—if you stay on the path, eyes fixed on Jesus, you will emerge into the light and see what God has promised. I merely don't want to see you blindsided, for opposition will come. So it is my prayer that this book will prepare you and strengthen you to withstand it. Did you know that the term *fairy tale* is defined by the Oxford Dictionary as "a fabricated story, especially one intended to deceive"?

Esther's story is no fabrication, so don't be deceived. Esther's mantle is a life laid down in service to the King of kings. It is less about her queenly role, and more about her heart position as a humble servant before her God. In a culture like our own, it is countercultural to lay down our life for another person. We are taught that our value lies in the praise and honor of ourselves. Images of red carpets are admired and exalted—desire for self-indulgence and self-worth are among our world's greatest ambitions. Fame, wealth, and fortune are today's values.

I'm sad to say this is true even within the church. Yet I believe the Lord is drawing His daughters in this hour into a place of consecration, of lives laid down for Him and Him alone, no matter the cost. Are you willing? It's easy to sing the songs and declare to the Lord, "I will follow You at any cost," but when the mantle of His anointing rests upon you, you must be prepared for the cost of the call.

JARS OF OIL

This is the spiritual terrain to which we have been called, and I want to show you, how Esther, too, was called to a very similar spiritual climate. In Chapter 1, we are given a few clues as to what she was contending with when she was called forth. Let's read Esther 1:1-3 (NIV):

> *This is what happened during the time of Xerxes* [Aha-suerus], *the Xerxes* [Ahasuerus] *who ruled over 127 provinces stretching from India to Cush: At that time King Xerxes* [Ahasuerus] *reigned from his royal throne in the citadel of Susa, and in the third year of his reign he gave a banquet for all his nobles and officials. The military leaders of Persia and Media, the princes, and the nobles of the provinces were present.*

From the foundations of this book, the writer of Esther (believed to be Mordecai) immediately lays out the spiritual landscape by informing us who was ruling over the high places. He writes, *"The military leaders of Persia and Media, the princes, and the nobles of the provinces."* Why did he only mention the regions of Persia and Media though? He was strategically informing us just *what* the culture was like, and *who* was sitting in these high places of prominence. *Persia* means "land of divisions," and *Media* means "middle land." The people of Media (or more correctly translated Medes) were descendants of Japheth, one of Noah's three sons. *Japheth* means "wide spreading."

These three definitions combined paint a prophetic picture of the cultural and spiritual layout of the land where Esther would be crowned. Whether these meanings were literal for the time they were living in or prophetic in nature, these names were singled out, I believe, to give us insight into our own day today. A land of divisions speaks today of the fierce opposition among the people. Then there were those who lived in the middle ground, neither here nor there. This speaks today of the silent, lukewarm church, the ones that refuse to confront evil and would prefer to stay on the middle ground so as not to offend anyone. Then we see that the divisions will be widespread. When I read these definitions, I am reminded of Paul's words to Timothy in his second letter to Timothy:

> *But mark this: There will be terrible times in the last days. People will be lovers of themselves, lovers of money, boastful, proud, abusive, disobedient to their parents, ungrateful, holy, without love, unforgiving, slanderous, without self-control, brutal, not lovers of the good, treacherous, rash, conceited, lovers of pleasure rather than lovers of God—having a form of godliness*

but denying its power. Have nothing to do with such people (**2 Timothy 3:1-5 NIV**).

The first four verses describe Persia, a land of divisions. The fifth verse describes Medes, the middle land, and with both we are given a strong warning: *Have nothing to do with such people.* We can certainly pray for them, witness, and share the love of Christ with them, but the moment we begin to converge lives with them, we run the risk of living spiritually in a place called "middle land," or "lukewarm." Or rather, idol worship. What's fascinating, however, is Scripture also tells us that King Ahasuerus's throne was positioned within the fortress of Susa, and we are informed in Esther 2:5 that this is also where Esther lived.

As you will have come to learn with me, I like to dig a little deeper than surface value. So if you will bear with me for just a moment, I want to take you into a side study of Susa.[2] I must highlight an intriguing detail about the etymology of the name of this Persian city, Susa. It can be translated to mean white or alabaster. Alabaster was a white, translucent and costly stone in ancient biblical times and this is a worthy note to pay attention to regarding the fortress where Esther lived. Allow me to show you how.

Alabaster is not a material largely talked about in our modern day; however, in the times of Jesus alabaster was incredibly valuable. This was considered such a precious stone that it was used in the decoration of Solomon's temple. It is a pure but moldable stone, and it was common within the Jewish culture to mold jars out of alabaster that store precious oils and perfumes. Alabaster was strong enough to contain any oil or perfume within it, therefore keeping its contents pure and untainted from spoiling. Alabaster jars were sealed shut with a wax seal, and to retrieve the perfume or oil, the jar would be broken. This leads us to the story of the woman and the alabaster jar in the New Testament. There are three separate anointings leading up to Jesus's crucifixion; three different women broke open alabaster jars of perfume and poured it out upon His feet or head. I want to highlight the one found in Matthew 26:6-13 (BSB):

> *While Jesus was in Bethany in the home of Simon the Leper, a woman came to Him with an alabaster jar of expensive perfume, which she poured on His head as He reclined at the table. When the disciples saw this, they were indignant and asked, "Why this waste? This perfume could have been sold at a high price, and the money given to the poor." Aware of this, Jesus asked, "Why are you bothering this woman? She has done a beautiful deed to Me. The poor you will always have with you but you will not always have Me. By pouring this perfume on Me, she has prepared My body for burial. Truly I tell you, wherever this gospel is preached in all the world, what she has done will also be told in memory of her."*

This story is among my favorites in the New Testament. While it may not seem like an obvious connection to Esther, this story is deeply intertwined with Esther's mantle. This woman broke open her perfume jar upon the head of Jesus, she counted the cost. Belittled by those around her, she knew what she was doing—it was an offering poured out upon the Messiah.

I have read several commentaries written about this occasion and all have stated how the perfume would have been so potent the aroma would have powerfully filled the house they were in, which is what likely offended the disciples. A life in deep surrender often offends those who are not surrendered to the same degree. What's more, the perfume would have remained on Jesus as He went to the Cross days later.

Let's pause on this event for a moment. The sacrifice of this woman breaking open her jar and pouring it out upon Jesus released a fragrance that covered Him and carried Him to the Cross. Is it possible that every time He felt overwhelmed with the magnitude and horrors of the crucifixion, that He would smell a trace of her fragrance—and the beauty of her sacrifice to Him encouraged Him to continue in His own sacrifice? It's quite possible. There is something profound about pouring out our lives upon Him that releases a fragrance to Him.

When you consider that Esther was living in a place called "Susa" or loosely translated, "alabaster," it signifies that hers is a calling that requires us to also lay down our lives as a sacrifice to Him. It is indeed a high call to pour out our lives upon Him; but it is a fragrance I believe that will be carried into eternity. Furthermore, Jesus said to His disciples, *"Truly I tell you, wherever this gospel is preached in all the world, what she has done will also be told in memory of her."* In a similar way, we see this same effect with Esther. Her story has been told from generation to generation, but when we look closely enough, it's not about her heroism, but more about her sacrifice. She laid down her life, and that is precisely what the alabaster jar signifies.

There is no mistake that Esther was positioned in the fortress of Susa, as I believe the Lord wanted this to be understood—to walk in her mantle is to walk in surrender. It is this position of surrender that becomes as an immovable fortress of love to the King.

In this chapter's reading of the book of Esther (Esther 2:11-14), you may remember where it describes the process that Esther had to go through once she was taken from her home into the king's quarters. Verse 12 (CSB) says, *"During the year before each young woman's turn to go to King Ahasuerus, the harem regulation required her to receive beauty treatments with oil of myrrh for six months and then with perfumes and cosmetics for another six months."* Notice she was required to receive oil and perfumes for a year. She was undergoing the very transformation into an alabaster jar. A vessel that would carry His oil and glory for the days ahead. It is that very oil that gave her strength to go before the king, it is that very perfume that carried her with courage to expose the plans of Haman.

Esther is an illustration of what it takes to give our all *for* Him and *to* Him. Consider how Susa additionally means "lily" or "rose." In Song of Songs, we find a prophetic picture of Jesus talking to His bride. I want you to see how the Shulamite represents you and me, and the song of the Shepherd King is Jesus speaking to us, here He confirms that we are like the fortress of Susa, surrounded by thorns, but in Him, we remain pure.

Song of Songs 2:1-2 (TPT) reads:

> *The Shulamite: I am truly his rose, the very theme of his song. I'm overshadowed by his love, like a lily growing in the valley!*

The Shepherd-King: Yes, you are my darling companion. You stand out from all the rest. For though the thorns surround you, you remain as pure as a lily, more than all the others.

Esther was a lily among thorns. The Persian world around her may have depicted chaos and violence, but she was firmly positioned, heart abandoned to the Lord. While our own culture today is filled with the thorns of death and destruction, I want you to observe how God has positioned you with the mantle of Esther resting upon you, secure in the fortress of His Son. You are an alabaster jar filled with the fragrance of your surrender that will release the scent of healing to those around you.

NOTES

1. My paraphrase of my own writing from Abby Johnson's book *Unplanned: The Dramatic True Story of a Former Planned Parenthood Leader's Eye-Opening Journey across the Life Line* (Carol Stream, IL: Tyndale Momentum, 2011).

2. "Susa Meaning," Abarim Publications; https://www.abarim -publications.com/Meaning/Susa.html; accessed April 11, 2024.

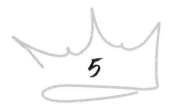

A STAR
IN THE NIGHT

She sits in the high places; she walks the halls of government; she is writing policy and legislation; she is instructing your children in education. She is emasculating men and destroying women with one breath; she demands for the blood of the innocents, and she has made sexuality the crux that beckons the masses to bow to her. She is full of pride and lust and convinces the world that hers is a pursuit worthy of sacrifice. She is introducing destructive ideologies, she is singing alluring tunes, inviting millions of children to sing along; she is seducing a generation; she is an enchantress. Who is she? She is the goddess Ishtar, the contrary spirit that is hostile to everything pure—she is the underworld's inferior imitation of Esther.

In his book *Return of the Gods,* Jonathan Cahn speaks of this satanic principality from Scripture, along with others. They are not just some ancient mysticism, but are very real and present in our day. Messianic Jewish Rabbi and Pastor Jonathan Cahn writes:

> The gods have returned. The ancients had exiled them. They wandered the barren and desolate places, the deserts and wildernesses, the alleyways and ruins, the graves and sepulchers. They haunted the underground, the dark realms of the forbidden, the taboo, and the dead. They inhabited the shadows of the outer darkness. In their days of glory, they had reigned over tribes and nations, kingdoms and empires. They had subjugated cultures and mastered civilizations, infusing them with their spirits, saturating them with their images, possessing them. They sat enthroned in marble temples and shrines of wood and stone, by hallowed trees and rivers, in sacred groves, and in mountaintop sanctuaries. Their statues and carved images looked down at their worshippers who approached their altars with offerings and tributes, sacrifices and blood, even human victims. Kings bowed down before them, priests sang their praises and performed their rituals, armies set off to war and laid cities to waste in their names, and children, the rich and the powerful, the free and the slave alike exalted them, worshipped them, entreated their favor, invoked their powers, danced to the drumbeat of their festivals, dreamed of them, loved them, served them, dreaded them, became entranced and seized by them. But the days of their dominion came to an end. They were expelled from the high places, banished from the palaces of kings, driven out

of the public squares, cast out of their temples, and removed from the lives of their subjects.

The gods could not rule over the modern world as they had over the ancient, not in the same way. But they would rule over it. They would not return to the high places and groves or to their ancient shrines and temples. They would inhabit the new seats of power by which the modern world was led and make of them their thrones. They would come upon the movers and influencers of modern culture and make of them their instruments. To gain dominion over the modern world, they could not appear as they had in ancient times. Though there was still a remnant of those who worshipped them and who called them by name, they were of the fringe....[1]

When we read of an idol, the picture of a golden statue may come to mind. When we hear of Buddha, for example, we immediately envision a man with a fat belly sitting cross-legged. Or when we hear Baal, we think of a golden calf. We don't consider the ramifications that behind these ancient, dead statues are very real demonic principalities that are still operating in our world today, just with different tactics. When we read the Scriptures, and what Rabbi Jonathan is speaking of, these powers of darkness sound foreign and distant. Because for the most part within our Western culture, it is not typical to see idols sitting amid our streets and thoroughfares.

When Nate and I visited India some years ago, it was an enormous shock to our systems to see visible idols plaguing the streets. At the entryways of storefronts and people's homes, were little golden statues, surrounded by a myriad of offerings—flowers, seeds, and other objects that had been carefully placed at the feet of these man-made images.

Even more shocking to us was the sound of chilling calls to prayer that were blasted through the airwaves over loudspeakers throughout the day. They were not calls to pray to Jesus, they were a summons to pray to Allah and other false gods. The atmosphere felt thick with possession.

Could it be that within our Western culture, we too have idols sitting in the entryways of our homes, cities, and high places? Though they are not visible with the appearance of a golden statue, they are indeed there. I believe the enemy has played a trick on us about idols. Because idols are visible and tangible in Scripture, we assume we don't have idols in our own lives today. Yet an idol can be anything that allures our heart away from God, even in the smallest of measures. It doesn't have to have a physical form of a statue. Today, principalities have been given immense power by the agreement of idolatry. Let me explain.

Have we placed idols in the open doors of our nations? Have we left a door slightly ajar, a door that was not properly closed, and allowed in a procession of demonic principalities to consume our culture? In the United States, for example, when God was driven out of schools in the 1960s, a door was left ajar. When God was commanded out of government through the banning of Bible readings within government halls, the door was pushed farther open still.

Many argue that the separation of church and state was insti-tuted to keep God out of our government, but the reverse is true. Roger Williams, a minister, initiated this concept by stating that there must be a high wall between church and state to keep the government out of the affairs of the church.[2] Not the other way around. What has happened, however, is we have removed God from the high places of policy and law, and then the body of Christ removed themselves from policy and decision in law. This removal has trickled down into every fabric of society, tearing it apart at the seams. Society has convinced the church not to engage in politics, and thus invited the enemy to take over policymaking in our place.

God was then expelled from homes, out of marriages and families. We have torn down the barriers of protection that He designed for us—the boundaries of godly marriage, the protections of a father and a mother—and replaced it with lust, entertainment, and adoration of ourselves. In the vacuum of His absence, who filled all those empty places? The golden idols of success, wealth, sex, and fame. The golden idols of education and comfort. The golden idols of feminism. The golden idol of self. While education, success, and wealth, even sex are not problems when they are within the boundaries of God's designs, it's when they tear away from righteous and godly blueprints and we desire these things before and above Him that they become idolatry.

Notice how in each of these realms idols have taken up supremacy. Education: what should be the foundational teaching of children has now an idol sitting atop it that instructs sexuality to be the main focal point of a child's upbringing. Wealth and fame: Hollywood, the media, and the arts are all largely possessed with demonic entities at their mountaintops. Western culture has welcomed in, no longer with a door slightly ajar but with doors wide open, every god and idol of history past to occupy new spaces in our hearts, homes, and lands.

Jonathan Cahn goes on to write:

> The gods now dwell among us. They inhabit our
> institutions, walk the halls of our governments, cast
> votes in our legislatures, guide our corporations, gaze
> out from our skyscrapers, perform on our stages, and
> teach in our universities. They saturate our media,
> direct our news cycles, inspire our entertainments,
> and give voices to our songs. They perform on our
> stages, in our theaters and stadiums; they light up
> our television sets and computer screens. They incite
> new movements and ideologies and convert others
> to their ends. They instruct our children and initiate
> them into their ways. They incite the multitudes. They
> drive otherwise rational people into irrationality and
> some into frenzies, just as they had done in ancient
> times. They demand our worship, our veneration,
> our submission, and our sacrifices. The gods are
> everywhere. They have permeated our culture. They
> have mastered our civilization. The gods are here.[3]

THE MOTHER GODDESS

So this begs of the question, who are the gods? And why do we
need to be aware of them? If you were a professional boxer, would
you enter the ring to fight without first examining your opponent?
You are not analyzing him to become better acquainted with him,
but to understand his tactics, to know his weaknesses. This is not to

become infatuated with the enemy; rather to simply set our cross-hairs upon him (or her) only long enough to aim for the heart—to take him out in one clean shot. So, who are they then, these ancient gods now invading our space and culture?

I recommend reading Jonathan Cahn's entire book, *Return of the Gods,* to gain a deeper understanding; but for now, we are going to focus on just one god. This one god of ancient history has slithered her way, like a snake undetected, into our modern world and permeated our culture and civilization with her deceptive speech. She is behind the blood sacrifice of abortion, alongside another principality that you may be familiar with, Jezebel. Yet, this specific goddess we are aiming our crosshairs on is by far the most versatile, having taken on many forms.

In the Bible, her name is Ashtoreth, also Innana and Ishtar. She is known as the "supreme female deity." Interesting. Particularly when you consider the pervasive ideologies of modern feminism invading culture today. Ishtar, as we will refer to her, was known to draw worship to herself through the forms of love and fertility. Once more, intriguing characteristics considering today. Our world has become obsessed with love and fertility or in modern-speak: lgbt rights, love is love, and reproductive rights. Love is preached from the high places of civilization as an all-inclusive, all-consuming overtone. Abortion is announced as a human right. That is, unless of course, you disagree, then you are a hateful bigot. Do you see the irony? If you deny this god's demands of worship, you are not bowing to her in adoration, and therefore you are viciously and vehemently harassed and berated. Her worshippers have become her army. She sends them out into the realms of culture today, beating their drums to the summons of her blood-thirsty exhortations.

There may not be audible chants and calls to prayer being sent out through the airwaves of temple loudspeakers in much of the Western world, but make no mistake, Ishtar has loudspeakers of her own, demanding prayer and adoration through the high places of our world today. She is called the goddess of war. Have you noticed how her chants have infiltrated social media? Her loud-speakers are her subjects, and they fill the airwaves with chants of "Free Palestine," a declaration that in fact is calling for the complete destruction of the Jews. Pay attention to her noise, for Haman is her subject. Haman—violence, a multitude of noise and chaos—is nothing more than a slave to her.

Ishtar's calls to prayer are conjured through government; she requires blood sacrifice through abortion in law and policy. She screeches for devotion from her servants through sexuality, for Ishtar is the goddess of love and sexuality. She has transformed a generation to believe they are no longer made in the image of God, as male and female, for she petitions the desecration of all that resembles the Lord—dismantling His image into the perversion of her own.

She enchants for her devotion through music and lyrics, through movies and television. She is known as the "mother goddess," speaking to her slaves through the forms of subservient influenc-ers. Fan bases of celebrities just so happen to declare their idols as "mother," for they too have fallen whim to her surrender. Yes, the likes of Taylor Swift, artists taking the world and particularly the younger generation by storm, are mere slaves to Ishtar. Don't believe me? Just closely read the lyrics and titles to some of their songs. Swift's song entitled, "False god" for example. Look closely at the witchcraft imagery of this and other popular music videos.

Taylor Swift is not alone—there are many other enchantresses like her. Are your eyes opened?

Many wonder why they are facing ongoing anxiety and depression, look no further than the open door of witchcraft in hiding, singing enchanting lullabies into your hearts and homes. This is no time for fun and games, this is spiritual warfare on full display—and many are unknowingly leading their children right into the enticement of Ishtar's worship.

Like the pied piper,[4] Ishtar's slaves are leading a generation to the summons of her calls. Playing their music, singing sweet melodies through the flutes of their throats, making fun and whimsical movies with demonic undertones—children, teens, and adults alike are marching to the beat of Ishtar's drums.

For the record, no, I'm not demonizing these celebrities, we need to pray they have true encounters with Jesus and become true shining lights for Him in these last days, rather than spokesmen and women for evil principalities. Make no mistake though, Ishtar has hidden herself, made herself unrecognizable, and allured a generation. They don't know it, but they are bowing to her every fanciful desire. As the goddess of war, take note how wars are on the rise, how World War III is being spoken of, how battle lines are being drawn worldwide. Ishtar is behind it all. Her name means "morning star." Remember satan's name in Isaiah 14:12 (NIV):

> *How you are fallen from heaven, **morning star**, son of the dawn! You have been cast down to the earth, you who once laid low the nations!*

Yes, Ishtar is the work of satan.

So you must be begging the question, "Where does Esther fit into all of this?" Esther's name is of Persian descent, which was peculiarly drawn from the name, Ishtar. Esther's name means "star." She is God's war-time piece of opposition and annihilation to Ishtar. Ishtar is the counterfeit of Esther. Wherever you see Ishtar today is where God is leading His Esthers, as cataclysmic ammunition against her every defense.

God is sending His daughters—you—mantled with the anointing of Esther into every realm of society in this hour. Do you see Ishtar's decaying fruit in education? God is sending His daughters into education, robed with the mantle of Esther. Do you see Ishtar's deceptive lies in government? God is sending His daughters right into the very halls where policy is written, anointed with Esther's mantle. Do you see chaos abounding in media and the arts? The Lord is sending His warring daughters right into the heart of Hollywood to overturn Ishtar's influence.

Where Ishtar has set up her myriad of temples and thrones, God is releasing these places to Esther to dismantle from the top down. Ishtar will be exposed. Ishtar will be subjugated and thrown upon the hanging pole, with her decaying body left for all to see. Where Ishtar has raided the minds and hearts of men and women, boys and girls with open wounds of deception, the mantle of Esther will be released upon God's daughters as a healing fragrance to the nations.

FALLING STARS

The protagonist and enemy in the story of Esther is Haman. What I want you to see, however, is just how alike Haman is to Ishtar. I would go as far as saying Haman was one of Ishtar's servants. Just a handful of the definitions of his name include "a multitude of noise, turbulent rage, violence." We will be studying Haman more closely in later chapters, but for now can you see the parallels to our culture in our age? We are living in a multitude of noise, people are subject to turbulent rage as we have never seen before, at least from what I have witnessed in my lifetime.

Our heavenly Father has given us warnings and understandings about this time we are living. Concerning such, I want to briefly highlight Isaiah 59:14-15 (NIV): "*So justice is driven back, and righteousness stands at a distance; truth has stumbled in the streets, honesty cannot enter. Truth is nowhere to be found, and whoever shuns evil becomes a prey. The Lord looked and was displeased that there was no justice.*"

Was the prophet Isaiah seeing prophetically into the days of Jesus, and also our own? Truth is nowhere to be found for we are surrounded by a multitude of noise. There is a reason that Esther's name is heard everywhere in this hour. Mordecai's infamous declaration, "*for such a time as this,*" is spoken frequently in sermons and online, and almost every prophet is declaring "the hour of Esther," and "this is an Esther generation." The Holy Spirit is speaking— and He speaks through repetition. He is confirming to us through these messages, through seeing 4:14, and in a multitude of other ways that this is indeed the hour of Esther.

God is not overwhelmed by the magnitude of the problems or principalities we are facing, or the apparent power of these principalities, for He has prepared the solution ahead of time. I would even propose that the prophetic words that declare ours to be an Esther Generation are the reason that the warfare has intensified.

The enemy has seen it coming, and he has cleverly crafted a response of chaos to prevent the prophecy from coming to pass. He has intensified the noise to drown out the prophetic word. But as we see in the life of Esther, the very harm he intended for us and our children will be turned back upon his own head. In this hour, we will see the shooting stars of demonic ideologies fall to the ground and burn.

THE MYRTLE

The tapestry of God's details in the book of Esther, astound me. From the fortress of Susa, representing the lily and the purity of the alabaster jar, to the Persian meaning of her name, and then Esther's Hebraic name. Mentioned only once in Scripture we find her Jewish identity as "Hadassah" in Esther 2:7 (CSB): *"Mordecai was the legal guardian of his cousin Hadassah (that is, Esther), because she had no father or mother...."* Hadassah means a myrtle tree. The myrtle is a beautiful, fragrant evergreen. Which means it remains green in every season, even through the night of winter.

During flowering seasons, the myrtle tree's flowers come in a beautiful array of colors, from deep purple to blood red, to bubble-gum pink and pure white. The fragrance that emits from this tree during its flowering season can be magnified through crushing its petals. This points back to the alabaster jar that must be crushed to release the fragrance. Is it possible that the Lord is leading you and me, His daughters, through this crushing that is taking place all around us, to bring us to a place of complete surrender to Him so we can release His potent fragrance? I believe so.

What's more, the myrtle tree does not grow with just one trunk; it has multiple trunks, each growing up alongside another, holding each other by their root system. This too speaks of the bride of Jesus in these last days when every daughter is anointed to walk in the mantle of Esther, not as a single entity, but together, united for the cause of Jesus. We are a strength to one another, not in competition with each other. When you flower, other daughters flower. Our connection to one another is what makes this anointing strong—we become too great for the enemy to overpower. Our interconnected trunks are what withstand the storms and allow us to continue to flourish and grow; no matter the culture around us, we are evergreen.

The myrtle tree is also known for its bark, drawing from various minerals within the soil, depending where it is growing. The same form of myrtle tree can be growing in Australia, and another in the United States, yet their bark will look different because of the different minerals in the soil. This speaks of the beautiful diversity (true diversity) of the body of Christ. Your callings and mantles within this Esther anointing may look different from mine, and that is what God intended. It's all beautiful—and it all radiates the body of Jesus. We are each called to illuminate a different facet of who He is wherever we are positioned.

The myrtle was spoken of in Scripture several times, one of which was during the Feast of Tabernacles, or Sukkot. This feast, which is still celebrated today, is ushered in by Yom Kippur, which is the Day of Atonement. This is profound because the Day of Atonement, under the New Covenant, represents the completed work of Jesus upon the Cross. He became the atoning Lamb for all sin of all humankind. This day generally takes place around September or October of the Gregorian Calendar. Then the Feast of Tabernacles is ushered in after it. This feast represents the dwelling of God, tabernacling among us. It was a feast that God ordained to remind Israel of past events and teach them of coming events.

There are three feasts that God instructed the Israelites to partake in each year, and the Feast of Tabernacles is known to be the most holy of them all. With the atonement of the Blood of the Lamb now complete, God's people are now prepared for the holiest of feasts. Five days after the Day of Atonement, they were instructed to build booths or temporary shelters. This was to remind them of how God provided for His people in the wilderness for 40 years, where they lived in temporary booths. Amazingly, this feast coincides with the final harvest of the year, foreshadowing the final harvest of souls at the coming of the Messiah. Now, this is where the myrtle is mentioned, in the building of booths:

> And they found written in the Law, which the Lord had commanded through Moses, that the Israelites were to dwell in booths during the feast of the seventh month. So they proclaimed this message and spread it throughout their towns and in Jerusalem, saying, "Go out to the hill country and bring back branches of olive, wild olive, **myrtle**, palm, and other leafy trees, to make booths, as it is written" (**Nehemiah 8:14-15 BSB**).

The Israelites will build, to this day, a shelter made of sticks and branches, with myrtle and other leafy trees covering the entrance and roof. The families eat and sleep in the booths for the entirety of the feast. This is to bring to their remembrance how God dwelt in the tabernacle. It was also a foreshadow of the coming abiding presence of Jesus, the Messiah, of whom John told us, *"The Word became flesh and made his dwelling among us. We have seen his glory, the glory of the one and only Son, who came from the Father, full of grace and truth"* (John 1:14 NIV).

The word for *dwelling* in this verse is the Greek word *skénoó*, which means "tabernacle."[5] This word also means to live in unbroken fellowship with the father. I believe that the reason the myrtle graced the roofing of the booths is because Esther is a prophetic picture of living in unbroken fellowship with the Lord. She is a portrait of dwelling within the atoning blood of the Lamb and a prophecy of the end-time harvest—the last harvest before the return of Jesus. The mantle of Esther is the understanding that confronting the ungodly principalities of our day cannot be done without the atoning blood of the Lamb. We must dwell with Him, unbroken. It is by His blood that the anointing of Esther is released. I believe it also speaks of covering our homes (booths). Hers is a calling to guard and be a gatekeeper to the home, exactly what the enemy has been targeting. Esther will cover the roof of her home so that no demon in hell can touch it; she covers and protects.

The prophet Isaiah spoke of the myrtle twice, to indicate change was coming. He used the myrtle tree as a prophetic symbol for new birth in the midst of chaos. He writes:

> *Instead of the thornbush will grow the juniper, and instead of briers the **myrtle** will grow. This will be for the Lord's renown, for an everlasting sign, that will endure forever* (**Isaiah 55:13 NIV**).

and

I will put in the desert the cedar and the acacia, the **myrtle** *and the olive. I will set junipers in the waste-land, the fir and the cypress together, so that people may see and know, may consider and understand, that the hand of the Lord has done this, that the Holy One of Israel has created it* (**Isaiah 41:19-20 NIV**).

The mantle of Esther releases a fragrance that is both beautiful to the Lord, but also to the world around her. Her anointing releases life in places of death. Where culture has been left in ruins, destroyed like a wasteland by the thorns of Ishtar and Haman—demonic workings of principalities that, like a thorn, have squeezed the life out of the generations—the mantle of Esther will pour out the healing balm of oil that comes from her unbroken intimacy with Jesus.

She will cut down the briers and thorns, slicing them at their roots. The brier mentioned in Isaiah 55:13 is the Hebrew word for "nettle" or "stinging nettle." One touch of the stinging nettle will cause your skin to burn for hours or even days. The briers are the words of Ishtar that have stung and burned a generation of children, but it is the words of Esther that will release Truth and healing, for she is the antidote. Esther will restore the family and her mantle is an anointing to rebuild the home Ishtar has burned down.

HEALING FOR THE NATIONS

The late prophet Kim Clement released a prophetic word in 2011 that echoes into today. Kim was one of those prophets who was far ahead of his time; people mocked him, belittled him, and laughed at him, yet we are now witnessing many of his prophecies beginning to take shape, years after his death.

It always astounds me when the church expects prophecy to take place immediately. God is not a microwave god. A lot of His words are not instantaneous, and we are required to steward those prophecies. I believe that we are now required, as His daughters, to steward this prophetic word spoken in 2011, and now we must walk it out in 2024 and beyond. Many have tried to dissect this prophecy, and figure out who "the Esther" would be. I have seen words released that declare, "This particular woman is *the* Esther about whom Kim Clement prophesied." I would like to propose that it is not one woman, but the mantle of Esther that Kim saw. I believe he saw this mantle as one woman, but it was speaking of the bride of Jesus with beautiful big eyes, for she is beholding the Lamb.

I want you to read this prophecy, and in doing so know that it is you God is mantling in this hour. Every daughter, not just one, but every one of His daughters are being robed with this mantle, and we will together pour out the oil of healing upon the lands. This does not speak of only the nation of the United States of America. I believe the United States is a catalyst for this taking place worldwide, so don't write off your homeland. God has positioned you to likewise pour out the oil of healing, wherever you live.

Clement's prophecy:

> At the beginning of the restoration, as it begins, there shall be a woman that shall rise up. A woman that shall be strong in faith, virtuous, beautiful in eyes, her

eyes shall be so beautiful, her eyes shall be round and big, I have crowned her, says the Lord, as I crowned Esther. The people shall receive her, for she shall have the oil of gladness, for the pain and the mourning that has taken place. She shall pour out the oil, she shall pour out the oil on this Nation. God says, "Healing shall begin and then it shall flow rapidly, schools will be free from potential damage and danger, shootings and murder, drug addiction. Cartels shall be afraid of a woman! A woman, anointed by God, a woman set aside." God says they will say, "'We hated her, but now we love her.' For she will take the oil of healing and she will pour it upon the scars of those left and those right...they will say, 'We shall not implement at all, socialism.' Where they have said, 'We will make history without God,' NO you will not! No you will not," says the Lord. For God says, "This woman will come and pour healing oil upon the nation, and they will declare, 'it is well with my soul, it is well with my soul,' for the soul of America has been corrupted. The soul of this nation has been corrupted with bitterness and anger," and God said she shall say, "'No more bitterness, no more anger, no more division' and shall pour the oil that shall come from the Spirit of the Lord Himself."[6]

Allow me to make this prophetic declaration over you, daughter, you are anointed with this very mantle. Kim was seeing you and me, the daughters of God, robed with this anointing to pour out healing upon the land. You have been appointed for this very moment. When God was dreaming up the ages, He saw the ferocity of our time, and He chose you. He instilled within you the strength to carry His name into the fiercest, darkest places inhabited by Ishtar. One strike of your words as you pour out the oil of healing and declare the name of Jesus, will cause her to bow low.

You, daughter, are anointed for this. You have been set apart and consecrated; and with eyes beholding the Lamb, you will see these principalities fall all around you. Shine, for you are a star among stars, shining and radiating Jesus.

NOTES

1. Jonathan Cahn, *Return of the Gods* (Sun City, FL: Frontline, 2022), 12-16.

2. For more information about Roger Williams see "God, Government and Roger Williams' Big Idea" by John M. Barry, *Smithsonian Magazine,* January 2012; https://www.smithsonianmag.com/history/god-government-and-roger-williams-big-idea-6291280/; accessed April 11, 2024.

3. Cahn, *Return of the Gods,* 12-16.

4. Interesting story about the pied piper by Raphael Kadushin, "The grim truth behind the Pied Piper," *BBC.com,* 3 September 2020; https://www.smithsonianmag.com/history/god-government-and -roger-williams-big-idea-6291280/; accessed April 11, 2024.

5. "Dwelling," *Strong's Greek Concordance #4637.*

6. Taken from the Kim Clement Prophecy, "Esther"; https://www .youtube.com/watch?v=s3r7acidxno; accessed April 11, 2024.

THORNS TO CROWNS

BIBLE READING: ESTHER 2:19-23

In January 2014, I woke up to a sudden and unexpected cloud of heaviness that felt as though it was quite literally resting over my mind. The feeling was as much spiritual as it was tangible, for my head ached in restlessness with a dull migraine, and I could neither think nor see clearly. My spirit felt heavy and burdensome, void of any hope or joy, which was so unlike my personality and temperament—particularly given the joy I was experiencing. I had just birthed our second daughter, Sophie, only a month prior and we were overwhelmed with happiness at our growing family.

I had heard about depression, and more specifically postnatal depression, but I never suspected this was what I was facing. This heaviness hit me like a freight train that had appeared as if from nowhere. There was no warning in sight; no inkling it was coming. It was just there from one day to the next. In a storyline from the children's book, *Charlie Brown,* Charlie's little bird friend, Woodstock, is followed around by a rain cloud all day. Wherever Woodstock went, the rain cloud would follow. When I woke up that hot Australian summer morning, I was Woodstock; and the rain cloud, which more closely resembled an ominous storm, followed me wherever I went. Only mine didn't last one day like Woodstock's, mine followed me for one excruciating year.

In nature when a female animal is about to give birth, she becomes extremely vulnerable to predators. A wildebeest, for example, is known to give birth while standing up and walking forward, as she is unable to rest during her contractions and birth her baby in peace because she understands that enemy predators can smell her time of weakness. Lions will specifically hunt her in the moment when she and her baby are most defenseless—birth.

It's a horrific reality for wildlife; and in our spiritual reality, our enemy, satan, hunts in much the same way. He looks for moments or spots of weakness; and for many women, he will attack at a vulnerable time like new motherhood. When she should be filled with joy and happiness, he will attempt to fill her with depression and sadness. Why? The enemy hates when we birth new life made in the image of God.

If you are a mother, you might remember when your baby was a newborn that your mind may have been bombarded with scary or intrusive thoughts. Thoughts such as, *What will happen if my baby dies while asleep?* Or crazy thoughts like, *What if an eagle jumps through that open window and takes my baby.* The world calls them intrusive thoughts. I propose they are demonic thoughts sent to overwhelm, confuse, and bewilder a new mother.

Prophetically speaking, I believe you and I are in a time of spiritual birthing right now, when God is breathing new life upon His sons and daughters alike, but specifically for His daughters. He is mantling you with the anointing of Esther, and it is a time of new birth. You may have already been feeling a spiritual war raging in your mind and you're wondering why. Perhaps you have never battled against depression or anxiety before, and out of nowhere you're feeling exhausted and battle weary. Could it be that you are in a time of spiritual birthing? I believe so. Therefore, it is imperative you know how to keep guard over your heart and mind as well as the hearts of your family in this critical hour. Pay close attention to this one detail, the devil is *like* a lion, but he is *not* one.

> *Be alert and of sober mind. Your enemy the devil prowls around like a roaring lion looking for someone to devour* (**1 Peter 5:8 NIV**).

SNARES OF THE HEART

Esther's crowning was one such susceptible moment; on one hand, there was a mass celebration welcoming in the new queen. On the other hand, her crowning was also a moment of vulnerability, not just for her but for the king and the kingdom as they transitioned from the familiarity of Vashti, into welcoming the new Queen Esther.

Consider the first few weeks of a new presidency in the United States. There is an air of uncertainty. Whether comfortable in the president's role or not, the newly elected official's every move is watched with a keen eye of scrutiny. What will his first steps be? Will he serve himself or the people? A transition in authority is always an uncertain time, whether for good or for bad.

In this chapter's reading from the book of Esther (Esther 2:19-23), you read about the king's two eunuchs who had plotted to kill the king. This occurred directly following the celebration of Esther's crowning. It was a birthing moment, and the enemy was prowling, looking for weakness to prey upon. He found that weakness in the offense of two eunuchs who were also the gatekeepers of the king. Interesting. Their roles were among the most important of roles, to guard the king at his gates. And yet, through offense in their hearts, they became the very threat they were guarding against.

Why is this important? If we don't take the offenses and pains of our own hearts before the King of kings, we will end up becoming the prey and the hunter combined. Rather than guarding our gates, we will open wide the gates of our hearts to unrelenting attacks of the enemy. You see, the enemy searches not only for times of weakness like birthing, but he also hunts for heart wounds that he can use for an attack. We see this often within the church. Those who have offense or wounded hearts become both the prey and the hunter for the enemy. Rather than guarding the gates of the ecclesia (the body of Christ), they allow the enemy to whisper through the strongholds of their offenses and wounds and end up opening the gates to unnecessary attacks from the enemy.

This was true in my life. As the year of depression advanced, so too did the wounds of my heart that I had never dealt with. Like a volcano, they came erupting out of me, along with anger, bitterness, and offense. I was resentful toward everyone, and I was angry at the church. I had asked our pastors at the time to pray for me as I was becoming overwhelmingly consumed by this dark heaviness, and I didn't know what to do to escape the torment. Instead of praying, they told me to go to the doctor and get medication for anti-depressants. "You're just suffering from postnatal depression," I was told again and again by fellow Christians and doctors alike. "You'll get over it." Yet something deep down in my heart told me it wasn't just "new mother depression." It felt much more deeply ingrained than that. I was angry. Angry at them, and angry at everyone in my world for leaving me to battle seemingly alone.

A family member told me, "I always knew something was wrong with you," and then laughed with eyes glistening, reveling in my pain. Nate, however, was an incredible support, but he was working long hours, and it was all I could do to survive the day, making sure our two young girls were well cared for and looked after. The second he arrived home I would rush to my room to sit alone and just cry. Each night Nate would pray for me; but one night he walked in, and with tears in his eyes he said, "God told me I have to let you pray for yourself tonight. I'm right here, but I can't pray for you anymore in the way I have been, you have to pick up your sword and fight too."

His words were like salt on a gaping, festering wound. I felt abandoned by everyone, but especially by God. As Nate closed the door to leave me in the room alone, I curled up in the fetal position on my bed and literally screamed at God, "Why would You leave me in this darkness? You promised to never leave me or forsake me; but instead, You have abandoned me!" I was yet to discover that this was the very wound He was bringing to the surface because He wanted to heal it. Abandonment. It had been sitting in my heart since the age of five, like an open, rotting sore.

As I lay in a heap on my bed, now weeping uncontrollably, the Holy Spirit brought to my mind a forgotten memory in my childhood. I was five years old, an only child by my father and mother up until this point. (I have an older brother and older sister from my Dad's first marriage, but they lived two states away with their mother. So, I was raised very much like an only child.) This memory was the night my mother was giving birth to my new baby sister, Stacey, and I was left in a hospital waiting room, alone.

Both my mother and my father were in the delivery room together, and with no relatives living close by—all were either out of state or country—and no one to call on at the very last minute, they were left with no choice but to leave me in the waiting room as she gave birth. Back then, doctors would not allow a child into the delivery room, so their hands were tied. Thankfully though, my mum had quick births, and this time she was only in labor for two hours. But two hours left alone felt like a lifetime to my little five-year-old self.

Being an only child until then, I had been doted on with undivided attention for all my formative years. Now, suddenly, I was alone. You may have already detected the theme here—it was a birthing. The enemy looked for a moment of vulnerability in a time of new birth, and he found it with me sitting alone in the waiting room. I vividly remember being terrified and scared, sobbing in much the same way I was doing so some 25 years later curled up on the bed. I felt now, as I did then, terrified and scared and alone. As though reliving this memory in real time, I asked the Lord, "Why am I seeing this? Why am I here?" I could feel the familiar sting of this memory as though it had happened yesterday.

In the next moment, God showed me another scene from this memory. As I sat sobbing alone on a cold chair in the corner of the waiting room, a doctor approached me. Dressed in all white wearing his long, crisp doctor's coat and a stethoscope hanging around his neck, he had kind eyes and a gentle smile. With eyes locked on mine, I remember him approaching me and I didn't feel afraid. He came close and said with a comforting smile, "Now, what seems to be the problem here? Can I show you something?" He held out his hand for me to hold. I slowly and cautiously put my hand in his, and he led me to a nearby window. The waiting room was positioned high in the hospital building, and he pointed at the view of Mount Coot-tha, a mountain in Brisbane. The sun was setting behind it and its rays were splashing beautiful colors of gold and pink into the clouds above it. He pointed at the colors of the sky and then turned to me and said, "Isn't that beautiful? It was made just for you today."

I vividly remember looking at the sky in awe as peace washed over me. At that, the doctor sat me by a chair next to the window and reassured my little heart, "Don't worry, your parents won't be long now," as he walked off down the corridor. Within moments, Dad excitedly burst through the doors wheeling a hospital crib with a newly born baby, bundled up in pink, resting inside it. He walked over to me and introduced me to my beautiful new sister.

Back on my bed all these years later, I came out of that memory as though I had time traveled and relived it all (let me clarify, I'm not suggesting I actually traveled back in time, merely highlighting the intensity of reliving that memory). I then heard the voice of His Spirit whispering to my heart again. "Christy, that was Me, I was the doctor who calmed your heart that day. In that moment, you thought you had been abandoned and rejected, I wanted to show you that I have never left you or forsaken you. Even in a moment that you thought was insignificant, I was there."

Tears continued to stream down my face as I could feel that gaping wound in my heart beginning to heal for the first time in my life. What's strange is, I never even knew it was there until then. Now I recognized for the first time; that wound had dictated so much of my life. Maybe you have experienced trauma far worse, but I needed to share this with you to highlight that there is no pain too great or even too small that He is not in the middle of.

I don't know for certain if the doctor was Jesus Himself (call me crazy, but it sure felt like Him), or whether He spoke through a kindhearted doctor in that moment, but what I do know without any doubt in my mind, He was there in that moment with me. He was right there when I thought I was alone.

I was led to look up the meaning of the mountain that the doctor pointed to. Mount Coot-tha is an Aboriginal name that means "place of honey." In the very place where the enemy saw an opportunity of vulnerability with a little girl to plant the seed of abandonment and rejection within her, the Father instead established a place of sweetness, honey.

I am reminded of this verse from Proverbs 16:24 (CSB), *"Pleasant words are a honeycomb, sweet to the soul and health to the body."*

Over the coming months, the Father began to reveal and heal deep places of rejection that all seeded from that one moment in my childhood. All the abandonment I had been carrying had cast a shadow over my eyes with how I viewed God, and even myself. Yet realizing He was right there with me, began to heal the deepest parts of my soul, and over the coming months, He kept guard over my heart as He led me through layers of healing.

I wonder, daughter, are there places of rejection, hurt, or pain that have been pent-up within you for far too long in the far-reaching crevices of your own heart? Have those wounds caused you to see God as an unfeeling, uncaring man who sits on His throne without compassion or concern toward you? Do you find yourself constantly having to prove yourself to Him? Considering the loss of Esther's parents, I can likewise discern how the Lord positioned a man, her uncle Mordecai, who would be like honey in her life, amidst the pain. I can guarantee you of this, He has done the same for you.

Mordecai became to Esther as the doctor was to me that one afternoon—a place of safety and comfort. The doctor, like Mordecai directed me to look at what I needed to see. I invite you right now, take some time with the Holy Spirit. Put aside this book momentarily if you must, and ask Him to reveal any places of pain, rejection, or trauma that you didn't even realize were there. Invite Him in and ask Him to heal the tender wounds of your heart as only He can. He will direct you to look at what you need to see. When in moments of deep pain and anguish, He will show you that He was right there with you, guiding you out of the valley of the shadow and into His warm and comforting light.

MORDECAI, THE GATEKEEPER

Circling back to our reading from the book of Esther earlier in this chapter, you may remember something profound in this small but significant story. We find that Mordecai was positioned right in the place where the two eunuchs were guarding the entrance of the King's Gate. Let us revisit Esther 2:21 (CSB) together, which reads, *"During those days while Mordecai was sitting at the King's Gate, Bigthan and Teresh, two of the king's eunuchs who guarded the entrance, became infuriated and planned to assassinate King Ahasuerus."*

Bigthan means "gift of God" and *Teresh* means "desired and dry and severe." I perceive their meanings are pointing to God intervening in moments of the enemy's plans to assassinate what the Lord has instilled within you and me. God desires you, daughter, and He releases His gifts upon you in moments when the enemy intends dryness and severity. Like the doctor in my story, Mordecai was positioned as the gift of God in a moment of weakness, to intercept the severe plans of the enemy. He was in hearing range of the enemy's plans, and as Scripture goes on to tell us in verse 22 (CSB), *"When Mordecai learned of the plot, he reported it to Queen Esther, and she told the king on Mordecai's behalf."*

We must pause on this verse for a moment, because—as we have already touched on Esther's orphanhood in Chapter 3—if her own wounds had not been healed, this could have been a moment when she too could have become disgruntled. How? We must travel back a few verses to understand how.

Esther 2:19 (CSB) reads, *"When the virgins were gathered a second time, Mordecai was sitting at the King's Gate."* Why does this have any relevance to Esther's heart, you may ask? Esther had just been appointed as the new queen, and earlier verses describe to us that she was loved by King Ahasuerus more than any other woman who had been brought before him, which upon first glance denotes a whimsical fairy tale like that of Cinderella's. The poor orphan girl becomes the beloved wife and queen of her dream prince. However, this was sadly not the case for Esther.

When Esther was taken from the safety of her home with Mordecai, she was likely not older than 15 years of age. As a young Jewish girl, I can imagine that Esther would have dreamt of marrying a gentlemanly young Jewish man when she came of age, someone she could fall in love with and start a family. Those dreams would have been dashed the day she was carried away because of the king's edict to find a beautiful new virgin for himself. When I think of my own daughters, it's a horrifying thought. Not to mention her orphanhood would have certainly played a huge role in the pains of her heart. Afterall, it's only human nature to desire to be loved and longed for. Having lost the two most foundational people in her life, then being taken away from her uncle, she suddenly found herself thrust into the room of a lusting king. Hers is no Cinderella story.

Scholars believe that King Ahasuerus's harem numbered up to or even beyond 1,000 women. They lived solely in the harem with their one duty—go to the king when he called upon them. I think we can rather confidently conclude that this king, along with all his other illustrious possessions, owned a harem of sex slaves. Imagine sharing the heart of your husband with a thousand other women? Let alone, sharing his bed. Grotesque and stressful to say the least.

Now the king was attracted to Esther more than to any of the other women, and she won his favor and approval more than any of the other virgins. So he set a royal crown on her head and made her queen instead of Vashti. And the king gave a great banquet, Esther's banquet, for all his nobles and officials. He proclaimed a holiday throughout the provinces and distributed gifts with royal liberality (Esther 2:17-18 NIV).

We read that Esther was crowned queen, and immediately following the banquet in her honor, we read in verse 19, *"When the virgins were gathered a second time...."* Scholars believe this gathering was to remove the older women from the harem and replace them with younger virgins. We're talking full-scale human trafficking of young girls. Though Scripture doesn't give us an exact time frame, we can assume it was during Esther's transition to becoming queen, even if that's up to a year or two.

Can you even fathom what that must have been like for her? All her hopes and dreams of marrying a respectable man were disintegrated. There must have come a moment when she realized this was now her destiny, and so she gave herself to this man, trusting that God had a bigger plan. Then the king called for another round of women to be gathered. I don't think it's by any coincidence that this tidbit of information is included. During Esther's moment of birthing into her new role as queen, did it break her heart to see her new husband calling for more, younger virgins? I'm assuming here, but I am personally inclined to believe that this caused her a great deal of pain.

> But Mordecai found out about the plot and told Queen Esther, who in turn reported it to the king, giving credit to Mordecai. And when the report was investigated and found to be true, the two officials were impaled on poles. All this was recorded in the book of the annals in the presence of the king (Esther 2:22-23 NIV).

Mordecai was positioned at the King's Gate when he overheard the plot to kill the king. It's worth noting that in Scripture, everything represents something. Jesus spoke in parables, and we can often find hidden parables within Scripture itself. A gate within Scripture, for example, represents the heart. We can find a passage that speaks of guarding one's heart, as though it were a gate in Proverbs 4:23 (NIV): *"Above all else, guard your heart, for everything you do flows from it."* Is it any coincidence then that Mordecai was guarding the gate? Absolutely not. In this moment of vulnerability for Esther, Mordecai was guarding the King's Gate. If her heart and orphan wounds had not been healed through the safety and comfort of her own gatekeeper, her uncle Mordecai, it's highly probable that Esther could have become the hunter against this lustful king.

Rather than sharing the plot of the two eunuchs to assassinate the king, she could have allowed it to pass by, and thus seen the assassination of her new husband. Instead, she told the king—on Mordecai's behalf. She shared the news of this report upon the shoulder of the one who truly kept and guarded her heart—Uncle Mordecai.

Which leads me to reveal something to you about him that is so profoundly significant in the story of Esther; it's a detail that cannot be overlooked.

MORDECAI, A PICTURE OF JESUS

I believe the Holy Spirit is seeking to heal the hearts of His daughters in this hour. Hearts that have been wounded through the trials of life, hearts that have been bruised by the words of a father, father figure, or even a mother who did not represent God's heart well. Hearts that have been traumatized by the abuse of a man (or woman) or leader in your life. Hearts that have been abandoned by someone you thought you could trust. Esther was trapped, living in the abuse of a king who did not value her solely as his only wife; but rather, sought the relations of multitudes of women aside from her.

Yet Mordecai remained as a watchman at the gate where she abided. Daughter, the Holy Spirit wants to draw that pain and poison out of you and heal the wounds within. Like Mordecai, He is the adoptive Father standing at the gate of your heart, drawing you close in this hour. He is the Champion of your heart and voice.

I want us to dig a little deeper for a moment to find another revelation that happens to be hidden within the name meaning of Mordecai. If we go back in the book of Esther to where we are first introduced to him, we read in Esther 2:5-6 (CSB):

> *In the fortress of Susa, there was a Jewish man named Mordecai son of Jair, son of Shimei, son of Kish, a Benjaminite. He had been taken into exile from Jerusalem with the other captives when King Nebuchadnezzar of Babylon took King Jeconiah of Judah into exile.*

Before I show you this gold nugget of revelation, I want to first encourage you. When you are reading Scripture, don't just rush over all the details, take time to study each verse, investigate the meanings of the names. The Bible is truly a treasure trove of hidden wisdom if you take the time to seek it out.

With this in mind, I'm going to uncover for you the meanings of Mordecai's name, as well as his father's and forefathers' names, and then I will show you verses found elsewhere in Scripture that connect to these name meanings.

Mordecai means "crushed and oppressed." It also means "follower of Marduk," but that is a thought we will address in a later chapter. For now, we will focus on the crushed and oppressed definition. Take a look at these verses from Isaiah 53, which prophesy the coming Messiah:

> *But He was pierced for our transgressions, He was crushed for our iniquities; the punishment that brought us peace was on Him, and by His stripes we are healed. …He was oppressed and afflicted, yet He did not open His mouth. He was led like a lamb to the slaughter, and as a sheep before her shearers is silent, so He did not open His mouth* (**Isaiah 53:5,7 BSB**).

Jair, Mordecai's father's name, means "He enlightens and exposes." *"But everything exposed by the light becomes visible—and everything that is illuminated becomes a light"* (Ephesians 5:13 NIV). Mordecai is anointed to expose and illuminate the plans of the wicked.

Shimei, Mordecai's grandfather's name, means "renown and famous." *"But you, Lord, sit enthroned forever; your renown and fame endures through all generations"* (Psalm 102:12 NIV).

Kish, Mordecai's great grandfather's name means "a snare." *"Keep me safe from the traps set by evildoers, from the snares they have laid for me"* (Psalm 141:9 NIV).

This one verse detailing Mordecai's ancestry also tells us that he was from the tribe of Benjamin; he was a Benjaminite. Benjamin means "son of the right hand." The correlating verse to this points us to Mark 14:62 (ESVUK): *"And Jesus said, 'I am, and you will see the Son of Man seated at the right hand of Power, and coming with the clouds of heaven.'"*

Before I piece this all together for you, I want to highlight one other detail about Mordecai's tribe, the Benjaminites, for they were known as skilled warriors and archers. Mordecai was a watchman at the king's gates. It's also worth mentioning that at the gates of a city is where key business deals were made, court sessions were convened, and vital public announcements were made. The fact that Mordecai sat at the *king's* gate describes to us the profound importance of his role, not only with Esther and the king, but his role in keeping watch over conversations and legal issues taking place within the kingdom. Mordecai was an archer in spirit, keeping spiritual discernment acutely on guard and on target for any plans of the enemy that would be hatched at the gateway of the city and the king's court.

With that in mind, allow me to piece together Mordecai and his ancestry, as there is a hidden story in the reading of their name meanings. Collectively, the hidden message of Mordecai reads: "He that is renowned and famous—Son of the Right hand—will be crushed and oppressed, for He will enlighten and expose the snare."

Do you see it?

Mordecai is a picture and a foreshadow of Jesus in the story of Esther. This is fascinating because the name of God is not actually mentioned throughout her book, though we see her faith in God on full display. Her obedience to Him through prayer and fasting is also obvious, yet God is not explicitly mentioned.

However, Jesus the Messiah is clearly seen through the role of Mordecai, and in a myriad of other ways. Mordecai points to the One who would come, who would lay down His life for those He loves. Jesus carried our pain and oppression upon Himself, He was crushed upon the Cross so you, daughter, may fully live in the purposes He has set before you. We see throughout the Bible, both Old and New Testaments, there were foreshadows of Christ in each book.

For example, Boaz in the story of Ruth is a picture of Jesus; and in the same manner, Mordecai points to the Man who will enlighten and expose the hidden snares of the enemy. I find it so beautifully poignant that Mordecai is the one who exposes the snares and plots against the king, and later he exposes the snare of Haman.

Today, Jesus is your Mordecai, daughter. He is the One sitting at the gate of your heart, and He is on guard. He is a skilled warrior, and He stands with bow and arrow at the ready, to aim at the prowling enemy who would attempt to ensnare your life and destiny in moments of birthing. Jesus is sitting watch over your heart and enlightening your heart to the Truth of your destiny in Him. He is the Protector of your heart, just as Mordecai was the protector of Esther's. He is the healing Doctor holding out His hand to you today and saying, "Come with Me, I have something to show you, a destiny filled with honey."

FROM THORNS TO CROWNS

I want to prophesy over you: I believe in the coming days, weeks, and months, the Holy Spirit is going to lead you into a journey of healing with Him, just as Esther was taken through her time of purification. You may be saying to yourself, *I don't need healing, I'm good,* but I believe there are issues of the heart lying dormant that you are not even aware of, but He is—for He is the Searcher of the heart. He sits at the gate of your heart and knocks, and all that is required of you is to open to Him. You may feel tension or fear rise at the mere mention of the exposure of some of the wounds in your heart. You don't want to deal with them, and there's even fear of what Jesus might say about them. Can I encourage you with this—ask Him to show you where He was during that pain. Allow Jesus to go into those places to expose the hidden pains, and then heal them. He does not condemn you, He only wants to heal you. We need the body of Christ healed and whole so we can pour out His healing upon the nations.

Do you remember what Esther's true name, Hadassah, means? Myrtle. I felt to share this Scripture once more with you, this time, as a promise over your life:

> *Instead of the thornbush, a cypress will come up, and instead of the brier, a **myrtle** will come up; this will stand as a monument for the Lord, an **everlasting sign** that will not be destroyed* (Isaiah 55:13 CSB).

This verse speaks of what God is doing in the hearts of His daughters in this hour. Where thornbushes have surrounded you, pricked you and suffocated your heart, God is removing them and replacing them with the myrtle—an evergreen tree that is ever-green in every season.

Regardless of what you are facing, the Lord's promise over you today, daughter, is you are coming into the time of the myrtle and ever-green. No more will you be plagued by the thorns of the past, you will continue to grow and flourish with greenery. Regardless of the season, whether winter or through storms, you will be ever-green. God promises the myrtle will arise in the place of the stinging nettle, which points to Hadassah/Esther.

The Father is causing those things that used to sting you to become a place of healing, not only in your life, but in the lives of those around you. The myrtle has medicinal properties, and it releases a strong and beautiful fragrance wherever it goes. It prophetically points to emitting the fragrance of the healing of Jesus to everyone you meet. Remember the colors of the myrtle flowers? Pink, red and white. The myrtle speaks of the cleansing blood of the Lamb, washing you white as snow.

Daughter, Jesus is your Mordecai. Look not to the people of this world and their frailties, you need only to look to Him—and through Him, your healing will come. Look to Him, for He is raising you up as a myrtle tree amid a world of thorns. He is anointing you with the mantle of Esther surrounded by nettles; you will release His sweet fragrance to those around you. So arise and shine like the Esther-star that you are!

> *Arise, shine, for your light has come, and the glory of the Lord shines over you. For look, darkness will cover the earth, and total darkness the peoples; but the Lord will shine over you, and his glory will appear over you. Nations will come to your light, and kings to your shining brightness* **(Isaiah 60:1-3 CSB).**

the ESTHER Strategy

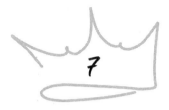

A MULTITUDE OF NOISE

BIBLE READING: ESTHER 3

You have probably heard of the spirit of Jezebel and how this spirit operates in our earth today, but it's very rare for us to hear or speak of the spirit of Haman, or Ishtar. Note: I want to first emphasize that I'm not suggesting that the man of Haman himself is operating in the earth as a ghost coming to haunt and taunt us, nor am I humanizing a demonic spirit. What I am saying is that the same spirits that possessed Haman in the book of Esther are the same spirits that are operating and prevalent in our world today—and we can identify these principalities by their fruit. I am merely naming Haman as a reference point for the demonic principality we are dealing with because his tactics and strategies are the same today as they were then.

I recently read an article by a Christian blogger arguing that there is no such thing as the Jezebel spirit or any other spirit like Haman, because they aren't explicitly mentioned in Scripture. To that I want to say, "First of all, what a lie; and second of all, this man needs to study Scripture more deeply." Demons are eternal spirits and therefore won't die until they are cast into the lake of fire; so the same demons and principalities that were at play throughout Scripture, are the same ones we are contending against today.

I will show you throughout this chapter how we are dealing with a very real and very powerful principality that used the same tactics through the man of Haman, hence why I reference this principality as the spirit of Haman. I find articles like this blogger's perspective to be extremely frightening, for they are setting up themselves and others for complete failure against an enemy who is highly organized and tremendously calculated. I would go as far to say that the enemy is more organized than the body of Christ when it comes to spiritual warfare, but I digress. Do we really think the enemy is just going to stop playing his games merely because we don't want to believe he's there? We either must wise up to his tactics, or we will succumb to them.

THE DEVIL'S SCHEMES

You have already read the word *principality* a lot in this book, and if you're not entirely familiar with the term, it might sound a bit perplexing. The term is mentioned throughout the New Testament, so before we dive into Haman, let's understand what we are dealing with in the realms of the spirit. In his letter to the church of Ephesus, Paul gives perhaps the most significant lesson in all the New Testament about spiritual warfare. Let's take a moment to investigate these verses together:

Finally, be strong in the Lord and in His mighty power. **Put on the full armor of God,** *so that you can take your stand against the devil's schemes. For our struggle is not against flesh and blood, but against the rulers, against the* **principalities,** *against the powers of this world's darkness, and against the spiritual forces of evil in the heavenly realms. Therefore* **take up the full armor of God,** *so that when the day of evil comes, you will be able to stand your ground, and having done everything, to stand. Stand firm then, with the belt of truth buckled around your waist, with the breastplate of righteousness arrayed, and with your feet fitted with the readiness of the gospel of peace. In addition to all this, take up the shield of faith, with which you can extinguish all the flaming arrows of the evil one. And take the helmet of salvation and the sword of the Spirit, which is the word of God. Pray in the Spirit at all times, with every kind of prayer and petition. To this end, stay alert with all perseverance in your prayers for all the saints* **(Ephesians 6:10-18 NIV).**

I want to bring your attention to the word *principalities.* The Greek word used here is *arché,* and it's from where we derive our English word *archaic. Arché* means "from the beginning" or "the initial starting point"; it can also mean "what comes first and therefore is chief."[1] What this is pointing to is a hierarchy of authority in the demonic realm, of "who came first." I often tell people who are trying to argue modern ideologies with me—for example, modern-day feminism—to explore the "origins" or "beginnings" and "starting points." You will often find that most of which, at the very root, are founded in demonic thought and precept—even if there are aspects of "truth" mixed in.

Another example is the sexual revolution of the 1960s. The starting point or beginning can be traced back to a predatory man by the name of Alfred Kinsey. The fruit of his teachings, though opposed at first, ended up becoming the foundation for the sexual revolution that claimed, "I can sleep with whoever I want, whenever I want!" From that concept, the idea of abortion was pushed and heralded by the masses, because they had accepted the idea that they deserved to have sexual freedom, and that also meant sex without consequences.

Paul used this term *arche* specifically to describe demons that hold dominion over things by order. In other words, when Adam and Eve fell, they handed their authority to satan, and the devil then passed down his authority to his demons, in much the same way an army is ranked. Demons hold rank by our agreement. They are also established in their realms of authority through "origin or initial starting points." However, these principalities are no longer in the first order of things, that's not to say they don't attempt to hold that position, but they were knocked off their post the day Jesus's blood fell for our atonement on the Cross. So, we are not facing a losing battle.

Colossians 2:15 (CSB) tells us what happened when Jesus died on the Cross: "*And having disarmed the powers* [rulers] *and authorities, he made a public spectacle of them, triumphing over them by the cross.*" The word used for rulers is the same word used for principalities, *arche*. Jesus removed their hierarchy and displayed His triumph over them, taking back the *first* position of authority. So considering Paul's teachings on the armor of God, notice he begins his spiritual warfare lesson to the church in Ephesus by saying, *"Finally, be strong in the Lord and in His mighty power"* (Ephesians 6:10 NIV).

The driving point being, Jesus has *already* conquered over these principalities; however, we must remain *strong* in the Lord and not in our own strength. Why must we remain strong? Because the enemy will test us, he will attempt to retrieve his place of authority by having us bow before him in fear or agreement with him. This is why Paul instructs us about the armor of God; if we're not correctly dressed and prepared for the battle ahead, the enemy will find a way to get in. Again, this is why we are focusing on matters of the heart (orphan-hearted issues) as well as the bigger perspectives of culture. Esther's story shows us that God led her on a journey of preparation so when the day of testing came, she was able to stand her ground, rather than cave to the weaknesses that once would have caused her to crumble under the testing.

I've seen far too many Christians become defeated through spiritual warfare because they are first and foremost, not taking the issues of their heart to the Lord. They attempt to wage battle in warfare in their own strength, or they attempt to battle principalities alone. Don't go into these battlefields empty-handed. For too long, the church has engaged in spiritual warfare with mere sticks and stones. We have entered a fight of the ages with twigs and pebbles, we have fought battles and lost, beaten to a pulp—then we wondered why. It is because we have not brought the mightiest weapon at our disposal, to the war—the Blood of the Lamb.

It's imperative not to give the enemy any ground through weakness. Principalities are not to be messed with. Without correct spiritual armor and divine strategy, they will wreak havoc on your life. While we pray *from a place of victory*, standing in the Blood of Jesus, leaning *into* His strength, we must also use wisdom when confronting these issues. There are hierarchies in the spiritual realm that need the entire body to engage in battle against. This cannot be won with one of us alone—it must be all of us together, standing strong in the might of the Lord's power and the Blood of Jesus. This is why, I believe, God is raising up an entire army of daughters, mantled in the anointing of Esther, alongside an army of sons, mantled with the anointing of Mordecai.

Before we move on, I want to bring one other detail to your attention that is found in Ephesians 6:11 (NIV): *"Put on the full armor of God, so that you can take your stand against the devil's schemes."* Let's look at the Greek word that Paul used for *schemes*, which is *methodeia*.[2] *Methodeia* is where our English word *method* is drawn, and it means just as it sounds, a "predictable, pre-set method." An explanation from Strong's Concordance describes this word to mean "used in organized evil-doing (well-crafted trickery)." Did you catch that? A pre-set method. This tells us that the enemy repeats his methods or schemes and they are pre-set, which means we can look for the fruit of what is playing out before us and recognize the method—and strategize ahead accordingly.

When we put on the full armor of God, we can see, strategize, and wage effective warfare against his pre-set plans. Satan's strategies may be well-crafted, but they are the same methods used over and over again. Which is why, when I mentioned the Haman spirit, I am referencing the same methods the principality of Ishtar used through the man of Haman and is now using these same methods once again in our culture, just disguised slightly differently. Let's uncover this disguised enemy and how he is currently operating.

THE ENEMY IN QUESTION

We are introduced to Haman in Esther, chapter 3. I want you to read the first few verses from this chapter as it immediately sets up some of the enemy's strategies through Haman from the get-go.

> *After all this took place, King Ahasuerus honored Haman, son of Hammedatha, the Agagite. He promoted him in rank and gave him a higher position than all the other officials. The entire royal staff at the King's Gate bowed down and paid homage to Haman, because the king had commanded this to be done for him. But Mordecai would not bow down or pay homage* (**Esther 3:1-2 CSB**).

It is intriguing to me that this is the absolute first mention of Haman in the book of Esther, and we are immediately confronted with his apparent greatness, yet there is nothing to describe what he has done to earn such high esteem with the king. We're merely told, "King Ahasuerus honored Haman." Why? What did he do to deserve to be honored? I think it's strategic of God to leave out this detail, because we can conclude that he did nothing to earn this honor. Absolutely nothing. It's probable that he sweet-talked his way to the top; after all, this is a king who loves to have his ego stroked.

However, a key is found within the next sentence where it tells us, "He [King Ahasuerus] *promoted him* [Haman] *in rank and gave him a higher position than all the other officials.*" We're going to pause on that word *higher* for a moment, because it leads us back to the term *principality*. This is confirmation that this is a demon of high authority and ranking; what's more, it points to satan himself who has an odd and weird obsession with being the highest. Only because he covets God and wants all the honor and glory. I've talked about this before in my book, *Releasing Prophetic Solutions*; but for the sake of those who may not have read that yet, I will give you a little backstory into this interesting detail.

Isaiah 14:12-13 (BSB) gives insight into satan's history with God:

> How you have fallen from heaven, O day star, son of the dawn! You have been cut down to the ground, O destroyer of nations. You said in your heart: "I will ascend to the heavens; I will raise my throne **above** the stars of God. I will sit on the mount of assembly, in the far reaches of the north.

Satan was known as "the day star, the son of the dawn." Remember Ishtar? Same meaning. He coveted in his heart, the throne of God, which is interesting, because if you look at Haman, he had weaseled his way to the throne. While satan may be a mastermind, he's not as smart as the Lord—he thought to himself that he could raise his throne above God and the stars of God.

I'm getting a little ahead of myself here, but this element is too good to pass by at this moment. Do you remember what Esther's name means? A star. Isn't it just like God to call upon an entire generation of women in these last days, bearing the anointing of Esther—an entire generation of "stars"—and using His daughters to counteract Haman/Ishtar, hitting him right where it hurts?! It's like a slap in the face. I can just hear God saying to satan, "You think you can raise yourself above Me? I'm going to raise an entire generation of my daughters above you. I'm going to cover them in the mantle of Esther so you will be confronted with millions of my stars sitting high above yours!" God, in His acute prophetic foresight is robing His daughters in this hour with this mantle—the antidote for the spirit of Haman/Ishtar that would attempt to raise himself up high, but instead, he is being cast down as you, daughter, step into this mantle of Esther/Star.

Which leads us to the fascinating meaning of Haman, which has both Hebraic and Persian transliterations. It means in no less words, "unique, magnificent, illustrious, trustworthy, and a multitude of noise." Unique, magnificent, and illustrious sounds like someone with a pride issue, doesn't it? Appears an awful lot like satan, don't you think? Isn't it intriguing that "trustworthy" is thrown in amid those other seemingly impressive adjectives? It reminds me of an illusionist.

I grew up in the days when David Copperfield and various magicians were huge sensations. Some younger millennials and Gen Zs reading this will probably have no idea who I'm talking about. Yet, I remember watching some of the magic shows with my dad and at the end of every program, we were left mesmerized asking, "How did they do it?" I doubt these illusionists would have had the same success in our day and age where we can promptly type into the internet search bar, "How did the magician make an elephant disappear?" Yet, all those years ago (I sound old), it was all the rage, and no one could figure out how they performed the illusions. Years later we discovered that each of the illusions were carried out with precision through alteration of the audience's perspective.

In the case where David Copperfield seemingly made the Statue of Liberty disappear in front of a live audience, he strategically positioned two large pillars on either side of the statue that held the curtain covering the statue. When the curtain was removed, the Statue of Liberty had disappeared, vanished into thin air. When in reality, the pillars were strategic diversions; and when the curtain went up, David simply (or not so simply) moved the entire stage, ultimately changing the audience's perspective who were sitting upon it. The Statue of Liberty had not disappeared, the perspective of the audience had changed to where one of the pillars blocked their view of the statue, creating the impressive illusion that it had evaporated into thin air.

I believe that the definition of Haman's name meaning trust-worthy is like that of an illusionist. What is most intriguing about the Statue of Liberty illusion is how David Copperfield made sure that an entire audience were unaware they were being physically moved. Surely they felt the tremblings of the stage beneath them moving, right? Well, not exactly. It was later revealed that he used the vibrations of loud music and noise to distract them from the ground beneath them moving. What's more, he did so slowly. The people were more intrigued with what was taking place in front of them, so they were completely unaware their position had changed. In light of that, I want you to notice the other definition of Haman—a multitude of noise. The spirit of Haman uses loud noise to distract its victims to the point that they are unaware, first of all, of the truth, and second, that they have been moved to a position of danger.

Moving on to Haman's father's name, Hammedatha, we get an even closer look at this principality. *Hammedatha* means "he that troubles the law." The Haman spirit is a stronghold that resists law and order, and I don't think we have to dig too far into the culture of our day to recognize this in operation in our world. In 2020, we witnessed this en-masse where streets were vandalized, police were demonized, and law and order was deemed as tyrannical. Democratic states across the United States have since upended law and order and diminished their police departments. In California, for example, left-leaning legislators changed the law significantly by introducing new regulations that redefine what substitutes as shoplifting or theft. Anyone can just walk into a store, steal up to $950 worth of product and walk away without getting arrested or prosecuted for the theft.

Conservative states are not immune from this insanity either. Just last year while living in Dallas, Texas, I happened to be standing at the checkout as I witnessed firsthand, a man leaving the store with a cart (or trolley as we Australians call it) filled to overflowing with products and expensive merchandise—without paying for a single item. I vividly remember gold necklaces dripping over the sides, and he just walked out without a semblance of guilt. I turned to the cashier who was serving me and she too saw what happened, and then went back to scanning my items as though nothing had even taken place. With my jaw dropped I asked, "Did you not see that?" Her nonchalant reply was, "It happens every day, we can't do anything." While I understand a female not pursuing a full-grown man for a theft, there was a security guard standing at the door. He didn't so much as blink, then looked the other way.

Another outrage is the pedophilic laws being rushed through in states, including California and New York. While I'm closely focusing on the US because this is where I believe many of these strongholds have been founded through thought and policy, other countries are not immune from this insanity. Oceanic countries including Australia and New Zealand, along with some European countries are swiftly bringing in legislation that defies law and order, or I should rather say *God's order*. France, for example, recently codified the murder of pre-born babies in the womb into their country's constitution. It is now a "right" to be able to murder your child in the womb in France, all the way until the moment of birth.

Meanwhile, many within the lgbtq community are working fast and heavy to redefine "age of consent" for pedophiles, and prostitution "sex worker" laws are being drafted into states and countries worldwide to enshrine prostitution as a legal and celebrated form of work.

Pornographic material is being pushed into children's education across schools in the United States and my home country of Australia too, and many teachers are secretly drafting children into an ideology that they were born into the wrong body. This is indeed all the work of Ishtar. I could fill an entire chapter with this derangement, but what it all comes down to is the spirit of Haman, through Ishtar, has infiltrated our world—and like the illusionist, the enemy has moved the stage ever so slowly, so the audience has not noticed the movement. Through a multitude of noise and delusion he has removed the veil of God's Truth and like the frog in the pot that is slowly boiling, the world around us has slowly accepted his illusion as "trustworthy."

A HISTORY OF VIOLENCE

Haman was known as an Agagite, and at first glance it's a detail that we could easily overlook. However, this little piece of information is more integral to the story of Esther than many know. We're going to go on a little history journey together, back to the time of King Saul to really learn who Haman was and how this principality operates. We'll be reading from 1 Samuel 15:1-3,7-9 (CSB):

> Samuel told Saul, "The Lord sent me to anoint you as king over his people Israel. Now, listen to the words of the Lord. This is what the Lord of Armies says: 'I witnessed what the Amalekites did to the Israelites when they opposed them along the way as they were coming out of Egypt. Now go attack the Amalekites and completely destroy everything they have. Do not spare them. Kill men and women, infants and nursing babies, oxen and sheep and donkeys.'" ...Then Saul struck down the Amalekites from Havilah all the way to Shur, which is next to Egypt. He captured King Agag of Amalek alive, but he completely destroyed all the rest of the people with the sword. Saul and the troops spared Agag, and the best of the sheep, goats, cattle, and choice animals, as well as the young rams and the best of everything else. They were not willing to destroy them, but they did destroy all the worthless and unwanted things.

Admittedly, that's an incredibly harsh portion of Scripture to read, especially with the infants and nursing babies—it truly hurts my heart to read. It can be a struggle to understand portions of Scripture like this; however, I want you to consider that if you and your children and grandchildren, everyone whom you know and love were being mercilessly attacked, raped, harmed, and plundered by a neighbor and their family, would you not seek justice against that neighbor? Then, in giving them a moment of undeserved mercy, they do it again and again and again? Would you stand your ground or allow them to continue in their savagery against you and your family? This is what the Amalekites were like, though far worse than the brief description I have given you here.

While parts of Scripture (especially in the Old Testament) are difficult to swallow in retrospect of our culture today, it's important we look at what God requested Saul to do here. As savage as it seemed, under Old Testament law there was a reason for it. Then we must consider how Saul responded. Instead of doing all that God asked, he took it upon himself to make a different decision and spared Agag, king of the Amalekites, of whom Haman was a descendent.

If you've read my previous book, *The Deborah Mantle*, you may remember how Deborah's battle began with a similar history. God commanded the Israelites to remove their enemies within; and instead of following His commands, they decided upon themselves that it was more merciful to live among their enemies, rather than kill them. (As a little side note here, I'm not suggesting that today our enemies must be killed. Rather, recognize that under the New Covenant our battle is not against flesh and blood but against principalities. They are the ones we are targeting—demon spirits of high places. Our mission is to set their captives free—those bound by demonic spirits. I digress.)

In Deborah's story, the Israelites' decision to live among their enemies resulted in oppression, oppressed by the very people to whom they showed mercy. Saul, too, showed mercy to King Agag, perhaps because of some empathy he felt for him as a fellow king;

but even so, that mercy was not reciprocated in the end. The prophet Samuel was the one who ended up having to take matters into his own hands. First Samuel 15:32-33 (NIV) says:

> *Then Samuel said, "Bring me Agag king of the Amalekites." Agag came to him in chains. And he thought, "Surely the bitterness of death is past." But Samuel said, "As your sword has made women childless, so will your mother be childless among women." And Samuel put Agag to death before the Lord at Gilgal.*

It was the prophet who had to step into the scene and fulfill the Lord's command; but unfortunately, the damage of Saul's disobedience had been done and somehow Agag's descendants remained in the land. The name *Agag*, in its original Amalekite language means "flaming and violent." It suggests a hot-headed spirit that when it rests upon someone, does not think logically, only violently. Interestingly, to a Hebrew audience, *Agag* meant "rooftop" or "the highest point." Do you see that? A high place, and even more pointedly, it represents the home.

Furthermore, we see through his descendants that the principality of Haman has a history of decimation and annihilation. Wiping out the Jews was not a new concept for Haman as his forefathers had been consumed by this violent principality, in pursuit of destroying God's people long before Haman was born. Additionally, I want you to see the tactics this spirit uses to force others into submission; the spirit uses intimidation and the approval of man to cause others to bow and come into agreement. When Samuel confronted Saul about not doing *all* that God had asked of him, Saul answered Samuel in 1 Samuel 15:24 (CSB), *"I have sinned. I* *have transgressed the Lord's command and your words. **Because I was afraid of the people, I obeyed them.***"

If we jump forward again to the story of Esther, we are immediately met with the intimidation and fear of people—these tactics were used in the first few verses with Haman:

> *The entire royal staff at the King's Gate bowed down and paid homage to Haman, because the king had commanded this to be done for him. But Mordecai would not bow down or pay homage. The members of the royal staff at the King's Gate asked Mordecai, "Why are you disobeying the king's command?"* (Esther 3:2-3 CSB).

Do you see the intimidation playing out? *All* of the king's staff were provoking Mordecai to bow down. Yet, this is where it gets even more interesting. Amazingly, in Mordecai's genealogy, we find that he was a relative of Saul. Kish, being his great-great-grandfather, was also Saul's father. This makes me realize something. The battles we are not willing to engage in now, are the battles we will pass on to our children and our children's children. Saul was unwilling to complete what God had asked of him, and it affected the generations to come. I don't know about you, but I refuse to pass on any of my battles to my children. May it never be said of me that I was silent in the face of fear, and in so doing passed on the battle to my children.

Saul's disobedience to the Lord caused a new generation to have to take up the same fight, if not worse than the one he had to endure. All Saul had to do was kill the king, and it would have prevented generations of pain, heartache, and warfare for years to come. However, when the battle came to Mordecai, I love that he did not crumble to the same pressure as Saul did; instead, he refused to bow.

As Haman discovers that Mordecai refuses to bow to him, he is filled with rage. This spirit of pride and arrogance that devours him, explodes out of him—then suddenly he realizes Mordecai's ethnic identity. He puts two and two together. Mordecai's descendants were instructed to annihilate Haman's descendants, and as Scripture says in Esther 3:6 (CSB), *"...it seemed repugnant to Haman to do away with Mordecai alone. He planned to destroy all of Mordecai's people, the Jews, throughout Ahasuerus's kingdom."* He goes on to convince the king that it is not in the king's best interest to allow this ethnic group to go on living, and in verse 8 (CSB), he says, *"it is not in the king's best interest to tolerate them."* I want you to see something here—what Saul tolerated in his day came back to annihilate his descendants in the days of Esther. His act of supposed mercy was not reciprocated with mercy. What we tolerate in culture today is not an act of mercy. For what we tolerate in our world today will come back to annihilate our children tomorrow.

The word *tolerate* in Hebrew means "to let rest, to let alone, allow to remain, to pacify." You see, much of the church has attempted to pacify the world by coming across as loving and not aggressive toward sin; we have not wanted to appear as hateful or spiteful. Instead of confronting sin while loving the person caught in it, we have pacified sin. In doing so, we have passed on a battle to our children.

This violent principality of Haman will not rest until it has consumed every man, woman, and child in its path. What we have to understand is, we are not opposing human beings, as the verse from Ephesians 6 tells us, *"your struggle is not against flesh and blood, but against principalities."* Therefore, our battle today must be fought and won in the spirit realm—by the Blood of Jesus. Do you see the enemy's methods at play here? Can you see the multiple parallels in our world today with Esther's day?

VIOLENCE IN THE STREETS

I had a dream last night, and in the dream, I was writing this very chapter. I was studying the book of Esther, and I was reading chapter 3 where it introduces Haman. The threat of this principality is immediately established upon our introduction of Haman in chapter 3, and within moments he is on a warpath against Mordecai.

In my dream, I saw myself typing these two words into this manuscript and the words morphed as one: **Haman and Hamas.** I then saw the Hebraic meanings of these two names conjoined as one, "noise and violence." I'll explain more in detail about this in a moment, but I must also mention, this is not the first time I've dreamt of Haman.

In late 2015, I had a parallel dream to this one. In that dream, I was reading Esther 7:10 (NIV), where it says, *"So they impaled Haman on the pole he had set up for Mordecai. Then the king's fury subsided."* I then watched as the name Haman transformed into golden hieroglyphics, as though I was uncovering an ancient mystery, and as I watched, his name morphed into the name Soros. So the Scripture then read, *"So they impaled Soros on the pole he had set up for Mordecai."* I woke up so perplexed by the dream, and the first words that came out of my mouth when my eyes opened were, "What is a Soros, God?"

You may or may not be familiar with George Soros; I had never heard of him until this dream. However, before I delve into what these dreams mean, I want to expound first on the name meanings, as I believe, though it is pointing to a human who bears the name, it is speaking of the spiritual battle we are in currently that is not just similar to that of Esther's struggle against Haman, but identical.

Now in light of the horrific events that transpired in Israel on October 7, 2023, I would guess that you are familiar with the name *Hamas,* the military terrorist group that carried out acts of horror upon Israel. This word is used in Scripture and it literally means "violence." It's interesting that Haman's "agagite" heritage also means "violence."

Soros is ironically another Hebraic word that means "an urn or receptacle for keeping the bones of the dead." This speaks of the annihilating spirit that wants to wipe out not only the Jews of our day, but every man, woman, and child who represent Christ. Soros represents the antichrist spirit (not to say he is the antichrist, but rather that he is perhaps making way for the rise of the antichrist in these last days).

I want you to see why God highlighted these two words/names to me through these dreams. The Haman spirit is a spirit of violence, and it viciously opposes God's chosen ones, His people. Yes, even the Jewish people, for His promises remain through the generations. He has not turned His back on them, and He is in pursuit of their hearts. You and I, the Gentiles, are also His chosen ones, grafted in. I beg those who are angry at these words, put aside your perceptions for a moment (perception, remember, can easily be deceived by illusion, through an upheaval of noise and slights of hand). I want to peel back the layers of the natural and peer into the realm of the spirit together.

It's important that we do this through the basis of Scripture, not what we are perceiving or feeling in the natural. Our world is in upheaval, and there is a growing discontentment and hatred toward the Jews once again. You will notice this has happened through slights of hand, and a multitude of noise. Have you seen the hundreds of comments under every social media post with the Palestinian flag? People demanding ceasefires and "Free Palestine" commentary.

Do you recognize the devil's method at play here? It's the multitude of noise. Haman and Hamas combined. They have convinced the world through this noise that they are trustworthy (remember, illusion), but they (Hamas) are nothing more than an urn of the dead. This is not to say I support any form of death of the Palestinian people, God loves them too. What I am saying is, their blood has been on Hamas's hands. I believe in the coming days and perhaps even years, we will see the strength of their number increase, and their hatred, too, continue to grow.

What many don't realize is that hatred will not just be aimed at the Jews, it will eventually be targeted at Christians too. Many Christians are in support of Hamas, for they have been blindsided by a trojan horse that has made the world believe they are the ones in the right. Hamas says, "We just want our land back," when what they really want is a complete annihilation of the Jews, and they will stop at nothing until they get that. Raping women and children and then parading their dead bodies is but the beginning for this principality. It wants the chosen ones, including you and me, dead.

We are indeed facing the principality of Haman, but not just from one angle, from a multitude of angles. This is why in this hour, there cannot be just one Esther—it is imperative that every daughter steps into Esther's mantle. We need a generation of daughters carrying the mantle of Esther, stepping into the courage required of every one of us to see this principality torn down.

While this all may sound very overwhelming and even extremely somber, we have the hope and promise that it is not futile to resist and stand against these principalities. In my dream of Soros, remember, I saw the name appear in the verse that says, *"They hanged Haman on the gallows he had prepared for Mordecai...."* I want to emphasize that I'm not calling for the hanging of any person—I am calling for the hanging of an evil principality.

Yes, even in these last days, we are a victorious bride, and God has given us promises to wage effective warfare over demon enemies. Throughout the book of Revelation, while there is great trial, we also find great triumph, and one of my favorite verses, which applies to this battle we are in against evil, is Revelation 12:11 (NIV), *"They triumphed over him by the blood of the Lamb and by the word of their testimony; they did not love their lives so much as to shrink from death."*

Have we been tolerating demon principalities in our day? Has the body of Christ largely chosen to only focus on our Sunday services, without waging war against the enemy? I believe so. Like Saul, the modern-day church has allowed the principalities to remain out of fear of what people may say, and for false empathy we have not engaged in the battles around us. I believe this is why

Mordecai's words to Esther are so profound, and they echo with warning to us today as well:

> For if you remain silent at this time, relief and deliverance for the Jews will arise from another place, but you and your father's family will perish. And who knows but that you have come to your royal position for such a time as this? (**Esther 4:14 NIV**)

Let's find out how to tear these principalities down, including Ishtar, Haman, and every demon god that has invaded our territories.

NOTES

1. Strong's Greek Concordance #3180.
2. Strong's Greek Concordance #746.

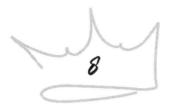

REND THE HEAVENS

BIBLE READING: ESTHER 4 AND 6

In the early months of 2010, I was in a spiritual wrestle for the life of my unborn niece. Her mother, my sister, Stacey, was just 17 at the time, and her early teenage years had been riddled with drugs and alcohol abuse, combined with physical and domestic violence of varying partners in her life. I've lost count of the number of times she almost died, and yet each near-death experience was intervened through the prayers of my parents, Nate and I. To describe in words the amount of stress this put on our family is near impossible.

My younger siblings and I had all been raised in the church, and we had heard on multiple occasions our father's testimony—of his own drug addictions when he was younger. God had rescued him in one single moment from a life of extreme addiction and crime. However, the enemy had clearly targeted my sister from her early teen years, surrounding her with friends who would lead her into similar drug addictions that my father faced. Then, at just 17, she discovered she was pregnant in an unplanned pregnancy.

My parents and I immediately intervened to offer our support, and Nate and I—newly married ourselves—offered to adopt the baby as our own if she felt the situation was too much to handle. Pressures from all her friends, however, suggested abortion would be the best option. Given she was only a teenager herself, with prevailing drug addictions, everyone other than us, screamed, "Abortion." She was the perfect candidate for the abortion industry—teen pregnancy, drug and alcohol addictions, instability in her life, a shaky relationship, and no stable job due to her lifestyle. One of her friends offered to pay for the abortion and called and set the appointment, just two weeks away.

During that period, our family wrestled and warred and prayed. I knew we were in a battle for the life of my unborn niece, and also for my sister's life. I was in exponential grief, soaking my pillow each night in tears as I cried out to God morning and night, begging Him to intervene. Stacey had been living at the time in between our parents' house and her boyfriend's, the baby's father's house. I would visit on the days she was at my parents and delicately attempt to talk to her, but she was resolute—the noise of her friends' opinions was louder in her ears than my voice. The date had been set and I was left feeling helpless, in bewilderment and mourning.

I can't help but think of this story when I read what took place in Esther chapter 4. Mordecai learns of the edict set by Haman, and he and the Jews fast, weep, lament, and put on ashes. I cannot even fathom the anguish of learning of not just one death sentence, but an entire generation that would be wiped out in a single day. Not only your own life, but the lives of everyone you know and love are destined for slaughter.

I've had a taste of this pain with the death sentence of my niece, and I can say with utmost sincerity that it was by far the most painful, excruciating experience. The thought of my unborn niece being annihilated in the womb and I couldn't do a thing to stop it, was too much to bear. I woke up one morning, living under the weight of this grief and sorrow, and with just days left until the appointment, I heard the Lord say, "It's time to fast." Now you need to know that I had never fasted a day in my life up until this moment. I wasn't even aware of the power of fasting or the significance of it, but I distinctly remember the Lord leading me into a fast.

All those years ago I had little understanding of what to do or how to do it. All I knew then was that Jesus fasted in the wilderness and it somehow helped Him overcome the temptations of the enemy. So I quietly fasted just one meal a day for the next few days leading up to my sister's appointment.

REND THE HEART

I'm going to draw from the revelations of our dear friend, Lou Engle, who has led a generation of sons and daughters into understanding the holy necessity for fasting. Knowing him personally, we have watched up close how Lou gives himself to the Lord during times of Holy Spirit-led fasting. I can think of no greater teacher on the subject, so the following quotes are excerpts from his book, *The Fast: Rediscovering Jesus' Pathway to Power*, which I highly recommend to you in gaining a deeper insight into this, all too often overlooked, spiritual weapon of fasting. Lou writes:

Maybe you have heard of The Jesus Movement, that glorious awakening of the 1960s and 1970s, when people were being saved everywhere. Evangelism was so easy! Someone said you could have said, "Boo!" and people would get saved. A friend of mine walked up to two guys and asked, "What time is it?" They responded, "It's time for you to get saved." And he did! We have not seen that kind of salvation awakening since that period, and it is the great longing and dream of thousands that we would see another Jesus Movement and way beyond.

There are moments in history where God ushers in the masses to His Kingdom like a combine harvester brings in wheat during the harvest. But while the '60s and '70s were a great era of evangelism, it was not the first or the only Jesus Movement. As you might guess, the original Jesus Movement started with none other than Jesus Himself.

It is my conviction that the beginning of Jesus's evangelistic ministry, circling around His baptism, His forty-day fast, and His coming out of the wilderness in the power of the Spirit, was not an anomaly, but in some measure, a prototype of every season of harvest in history. They all follow this original pattern. When all the people were baptized, it came to pass that Jesus also was baptized; and while He prayed, the heaven was opened. And the Holy Spirit descended in bodily form like a dove upon Him, and a voice came from heaven which said, "you are My beloved Son; in You I am well pleased"... Then Jesus, being filled with the Holy Spirit, returned from the Jordan and was led by the Spirit in the wilderness, being tempted for forty days by the devil. And in those days He ate nothing, and afterward, when they had ended, He was hungry.... Then Jesus returned in the power of the Spirit to Galilee, and news of Him went out through all the surrounding region. And He taught in all their synagogues, being glorified by all. (Luke 3:21-22, 4:1-2, 14-15).

After His baptism and confirmation of sonship through the Father's voice from heaven, "This is my beloved Son, in whom I am well pleased" (Matt. 3:17), Jesus was immediately driven by the Spirit of God into the wilderness for a prolonged wilderness season of fasting, prayer, and testing. It was during this fast, the Jesus Fast, that He overcame the temptations of Satan and came out in the power of the Holy Spirit with authority over sickness, disease, and demonic oppression. Many would think that when Jesus was driven by the Spirit into the wilderness to fast for forty days, the weakness of His body during the fast would make Him more susceptible to Satan's temptations. In actuality, the fast strengthened Him in spirit and enabled Him to subdue the power of His flesh so He could overcome. As we said in the *The Jesus Fast,* "Adam was tempted with a full stomach in paradise, yet failed. Jesus was tempted in the desert while ravenously hungry, yet succeeded. Jesus was driven by the Spirit into the fast, not just in the weakness of humanity, but as the dread champion Son of

God. God was picking a fight with the devil through His own beloved Son. After gaining internal victory over temptation, Jesus went forth in the power of the Spirit with external victory over demons, sickness, disease, and mental illness. It was the Jesus Fast that unleashed the Jesus Movement! The Jesus Fast is one of God's weapons for overcoming the enemy of our souls, yes, the world, the flesh, and the devil. It is the fully bent bow that shoots the arrow of the Lord's victory over temptation, thus unleashing the divine destinies of the saints."

I could fill this whole chapter with Lou's entire book, but I encourage you to read it for yourself, as it truly uncovers the mysteries of fasting—and ironically, begets a hunger to engage with this spiritual weapon. I will be the first to say I don't particularly love enduring without food; however, I love the spiritual effects of fasting. As Lou also says, "History may be shaped in the halls of academia and power wielded by fools, financiers, and politicians, but in the halls of Heaven, history is shaped by intercessors."

When Mordecai learned of the decree that had been sent forth against him and the Jews, his immediate response was to mourn and fast:

> When Mordecai learned all that occurred, he tore his clothes, put on sackcloth and ashes, went into the middle of the city, and cried loudly and bitterly. ...There was great mourning among the Jewish people in every province where the king's command and edict came.

They fasted, wept, and lamented, and many lay in sackcloth and ashes (**Esther 4:1,3 CSB**).

It's difficult to understand Mordecai's actions in this very moment, because in our modern culture, we tend to withdraw our deep emotions and reserve them for seclusion. Yet in Esther's time, mourning and pain were displayed publicly. Putting on sackcloth and laying in ashes represented desperation and extreme grief. Furthermore, the tearing of clothes along with fasting displayed a profound act of sorrow. As I was studying these verses, I was led to explore the Hebrew meaning of *tore* in reference to the tearing of one's clothes. It's the word *qara,* and it means "to rend, to violently tear apart."[1]

I used to think that fasting was just the separation of food from the natural body, but what it really is, is the tearing of our hearts in desperation before the Lord. It's a prophetic act of separating ourselves from our natural world to set our hearts upon Him and seeking Him for the answers we need. If you are merely fasting by skipping a meal or two and not engaging in prayer, you are doing nothing more than starving yourself.

Let me take you a little deeper here. This word *qara* is also mentioned in Joel 2:12-13 (BSB). Within this chapter, Joel is prophesying about an army of locusts, a day of darkness that would come upon the earth when everything is devoured by the plague of insidious insects. Yet during such horror, Joel instructs the people of the Lord:

Yet even now," declares the Lord, "return to Me with all your heart, with fasting, weeping, and mourning." So **rend your hearts** *and not your garments, and return*

to the Lord your God. For He is gracious and compas-
sionate, slow to anger, abounding in loving devotion.
And He relents from sending disaster.

Let me repeat this phrase, *"return to Me with all your heart,*
with fasting, weeping, and mourning." Fasting is the recognition
that without God, our efforts are futile. When I came before the
Lord on behalf of my niece's life, I didn't entirely understand what
I was doing by fasting. What I did understand, however, was that I
was desperate—my heart, like the garments of Mordecai, had been
torn. I knew that either the Lord would intervene, or it would be
all over for the child.

Many see fasting as an act of something they can do to make
God move. This mentality is the opposite of true fasting. A true fast
is coming to the Lord in a place of humility and repentance, not
in "an act" but in humility of heart. It is the acknowledgment that
without Him, we are nothing. I believe Mordecai was displaying
a prophetic foreshadow of a more powerful fast to come, through
the tearing of his clothes—when Joel would prophesy within these
verses of what a coming fast would look like under the New Covenant of Jesus. It wouldn't be a rending of garments, but instead a
rending of the heart.

Rend your hearts, not your garments. Mordecai understood
that the people were in dire need of divine intervention, so the
entire population of Jews also entered a time of fasting and weeping. What if the times we are living in now demand of us our
own rending of hearts? What if, rather than pointing the finger
or burying our heads from the prevailing darkness, we fasted
and wept for our children over the death decrees that have been

written against them—edicts such as abortion, transgenderism, and the re-writing of their identities into sexual perversions? The time is long past that a loud lament must be lifted up before the Lord, where we tear our hearts open before Him on behalf of the generations. I wonder what would happen if we dared to rend our hearts in this hour. To quote my friend Lou Engle again, "We have taught a generation to feast and play, but the times demand we fast and pray."

THE FAST THAT INTERRUPTS THE NIGHT

Three days into my own fast, I awoke the day before Stacey's scheduled abortion, having had a detailed dream of divine instruction that night. My conversations with my sister had been futile up until this point, even breaking out in fights where she would storm out of the house in fury at me. The edict of abortion that had been written over her mind, like that of Haman's, had cast a spell of great confusion over her. Deep down, I could see her spirit wrestling, knowing the truth, yet the words of her friends that were laced with lies, told her that the precious life growing within her womb was nothing more than a myriad of lifeless cells. Attempting to tussle with her over the truth only left her all the angrier, and so I knew we were in a place of desperation.

The morning before her scheduled abortion, I woke up and gasped. I had fasted just three meals over three days, and in this one night an answer came in the form of a dream. "Could it be that simple?" I asked the Lord as I woke up reflecting what I had witnessed in my sleep.

In the dream, I had seen myself writing a list of pros and cons. Pros, listing all the wonderful attributes of the gift of life this baby would bring. Cons, listing all the lies my sister had been uttering on repeat every time we had conversations. In the dream, I had written a list of pros that far outweighed all the cons; each point I made addressed the lies in a simple way. Then in the dream, I went into her room and put the list inside her purse and placed it distinctly on the dressing table where she would see it.

So the next morning, I woke up and did exactly as I had seen in the dream. Shaking, knowing that this was a last attempt to save my niece's life, I finished the list on a simple piece of paper, folded it and wrote on the outside, "From God." Then just as I had observed in my dream, I put it in her purse and placed it on her dressing table.

The note read something like this (sharing from memory because it was more than 14 years ago now, but these are some of the things I remember writing):

Pros	Cons
You have a family who will help you every step of the way. You will never be alone.	"I am too young to have a baby."
We are going to provide for everything, you and your baby will never go without.	"I don't have enough money."

Pros	Cons
You are already a mother and trust me, as your baby grows, you are going to fall madly, deeply in love with him or her.	"I'm not ready to be a mum."
Your life has already been interrupted by drugs…your baby is going to save your life, not ruin it.	"A baby will interrupt my life."
You will never regret giving your baby life.	
Your baby marks a new season in your life, he or she is going to bring you so much joy.	
Christmas is going to be so fun with a new baby in the family, think of how he or she is going to love waking up on Christmas morning like we did as kids.	
I wonder what he or she looks like. I wonder if he or she will have your cute button nose that you had as a toddler?	

Pros	Cons
The joy your baby is going to bring you will far outweigh any fear you are feeling now.	

The list I wrote was much longer than this one, but I made certain to address every lie with the truth, then wrote a new declaration over this baby that far outweighed every lie that had warred against her life.

I didn't realize it then, but this simple note was writing a new edict and declaration in place of the one "Haman" had written over my sister and niece. My sister didn't see the note until the morning of her scheduled abortion when she picked up her purse and the note fell out. She opened it, and later told me that she wept on her bed as the lies broke off her mind, one by one.

She cancelled the appointment then and there.

I remember the day I went with Stacey for her first scan. As we waited in front of the building to go in, a double rainbow appeared over the doctor's office, and we both cried, knowing that God's promises had prevailed over both Natalie and Stacey. My niece was born later that year, and everything I had written about her was true. Her name, Natalie Grace, means "gift of grace," and she is the most beautiful gift of grace in our family. The enemy threatened her life for a reason—she is a gift of grace to all those around her, and I know in the days to come she has been marked by the Lord as a weapon for her generation.

In Esther 4:16-17 (CSB), Esther calls a fast in response to the urgent hour at hand. She says, *"Go and assemble all the Jews who can be found in Susa and fast for me. Don't eat or drink for three days, night or day, I and my female servants will also fast in the same way. After that, I will go to the king, even if it is against the law. If I perish, I perish. So, Mordecai went and did everything Esther had commanded him."*

I know everyone loves to quote Mordecai's words of "for such a time as this" from this same chapter, but I also love Esther's declaration in verse 16 just as much. Esther was rending her heart here, laying her life down before the king for the sake of her people. Could this be what a true fast looks like to the Lord? One where our hearts are in a position of utter and complete brokenness before Him, where we say, "If I perish, I perish"? Could the lives of our children depend on such a declaration and act of humility, where it's not about us and our desires, but about the lives of tomorrow's generations? I believe so.

Just look at what this fast produces. Esther, Mordecai, and the Jews rend their hearts before the Lord for three days, then Esther goes before the king. To summarize Esther chapter 5, Esther requests the presence of the king and Haman at the first banquet. Haman returns from this banquet with his head pridefully bloated; yet as he is making his way home that evening, he sees Mordecai at the king's gate. Noticing that Mordecai doesn't bow or tremble before him, Haman plots with his wife Zeresh that evening to hang Mordecai the very next day. What unfolds next in chapter 6 is where I want to draw your attention.

That night sleep escaped the king; so he ordered the Book of Records, the Chronicles, to be brought in and read to him. And there it was found recorded that Mordecai had exposed Bigthana and Teresh, two of the eunuchs who guarded the king's entrance, when they had conspired to assassinate King Xerxes (**Esther 6:1-2 BSB**).

What was it that interrupted the king's sleep that very night? Was it a coincidence that the same night a gallows was being built to hang Mordecai, the following morning the king was awakened and was brought to a moment of recollection of what Mordecai had done for him? I daresay, it was the people's fasting and prayers that tore open the heavens; it was the fast that broke open the heavenly realm over the king and caused restlessness in his spirit so that he would be awakened to the enemy's plans.

Just as I witnessed the veil lift from my sister's eyes, so too had the veil lifted from the king this night, and he remembered what had been done for him by Mordecai. My sister remembered the truth on what would have been the darkest day of her life. Instead of death, life and honor was afforded Mordecai that following morning. Instead of death, life was given to my baby niece. What's more, honor was bestowed upon Mordecai by his very enemy, in what would be Haman's final humiliation before his own death. Observe how the fast of humility will break open the heavens, humbling and humiliating the enemy in our very presence.

The king inquired, "What honor or dignity has been bestowed on Mordecai for this act?" "Nothing has been done for him," replied the king's attendants. "Who is in the court?" the king asked.

Now Haman had just entered the outer court of the palace to ask the king to hang Mordecai on the gallows he had prepared for him. So the king's attendants answered him, "Haman is there, standing in the court." "Bring him in," ordered the king. Haman entered, and the king asked him, "What should be done for the man whom the king is delighted to honor?" Now Haman thought to himself, "Whom would the king be delighted to honor more than me?"

And Haman told the king, "For the man whom the king is delighted to honor, have them bring a royal robe that the king himself has worn and a horse on which the king himself has ridden—one with a royal crest placed on its head. Let the robe and the horse be entrusted to one of the king's most noble princes. Let them array the man the king wants to honor and parade him on the horse through the city square, proclaiming before him, 'This is what is done for the man whom the king is delighted to honor!'"

"Hurry," said the king to Haman, "and do just as you proposed. Take the robe and the horse to Mordecai the Jew, who is sitting at the king's gate. Do not neglect anything that you have suggested." So Haman took the robe and the horse, arrayed Mordecai, and paraded him through the city square, crying out before him, "This is what is done for the man whom the king is delighted to honor!"

Then Mordecai returned to the king's gate. But Haman rushed home, with his head covered in grief. Haman told his wife Zeresh and all his friends everything that had happened. His advisers and his wife Zeresh said to him, "Since Mordecai, before whom your downfall has begun, is Jewish, you will not prevail against him—for surely you will fall before him." While they were still speaking with Haman, the king's eunuchs arrived and rushed him to the banquet that Esther had prepared (Esther 6:3-14 BSB).

Are you feeling the conviction of the Holy Spirit as I am in this hour? I believe the Lord is leading us, His bride, into times of fasting and repentance. Times when we throw away everything that entangles and distracts us from Him, and we fix our eyes on the only One who can fix everything.

BREAK OPEN THE HEAVENS

In Mark 1:10 (NIV) we find the description of the baptism of Jesus, *"Just as Jesus was coming up out of the water, he saw heaven being torn open and the Spirit descending on him like a dove."* The word Mark used in this text for "torn open" is the Greek word *shizo;* and you guessed it, it indeed means "to rend, to divide, to asunder." This is astonishing. Jesus had not even walked into the wilderness yet, nor had He entered the fast. Yet the heavens had torn open *before* He even fasted.

Jesus was setting a new precedent. He was revealing to us that the surrender of His life through the baptism of the Holy Spirit would rend the heavens, and *before* He entered the wilderness to fast, the Holy Spirit would empower Him to do so. When He later died upon the Cross, Luke 23:45 (BSB) tells us, *"The sun was darkened, and the veil of the temple was torn down the middle."* The word for *torn* is indeed *shizo,* to rend. The veil was broken and split in two; therefore, our access to everything we need within the presence of God was granted in full. This means when we engage in a fast today, we are not seeking an awaiting answer as Mordecai and Esther had to; rather, we are pulling on the heavens that are already opened. We are not begging God for a solution for the problems we are facing; instead, we are pulling on the answer that is readily available to us—the very body and Blood of Jesus.

The fast under the New Covenant is no longer an entreaty for answers but an engagement in the supernatural power of the Holy Spirit and the Blood of Jesus to overthrow the enemy in every realm of our lives. The fast is no longer the act of tearing our clothes, but rending our hearts before Him. I want you to read this promise from Isaiah 58 and look at the ramifications of a true fast—of rending our hearts before the Lord. Pay attention to what takes place:

> *[True Fasts and Sabbaths]*
>
> *Cry aloud, do not hold back! Raise your voice like a ram's horn. Declare to My people their transgression and to the house of Jacob their sins. For day after day they seek Me and delight to know My ways, like a nation that does what is right and does not forsake the justice of their God. They ask Me for righteous judgments; they delight in the nearness of God.*
>
> *Why have we fasted, and You have not seen? Why have we humbled ourselves, and You have not noticed? Behold, on the day of your fast, you do as you please, and you oppress all your workers. You fast with*

contention and strife to strike viciously with your fist. You cannot fast as you do today and have your voice be heard on high.

Is this the fast I have chosen: a day for a man to deny himself, to bow his head like a reed, and to spread out sackcloth and ashes? Will you call this a fast and a day acceptable to the Lord?

Isn't this the fast that I have chosen: to break the chains of wickedness, to untie the cords of the yoke, to set the oppressed free and tear off every yoke? Isn't it to share your bread with the hungry, to bring the poor and homeless into your home, to clothe the naked when you see him, and not to turn away from your own flesh and blood?

Then your light will break forth like the dawn, and your healing will come quickly. Your righteousness will go before you, and the glory of the Lord will be your rear guard. Then you will call, and the Lord will answer; you will cry out, and He will say, "Here I am." If you remove the yoke from your midst, the pointing of the finger and malicious talk, and if you give yourself to the hungry and satisfy the afflicted soul, then your light will go forth in the darkness, and your night will be like noonday. The Lord will always guide you; He will satisfy you in a sun-scorched land and strengthen your frame. You will be like a well-watered garden, like a spring whose waters never fail. Your people will rebuild the ancient ruins; you will restore the age-old foundations; you will be called Repairer of the Breach, Restorer of the Streets of Dwelling.

If you turn your foot from breaking the Sabbath, from doing as you please on My holy day, if you call the Sabbath a delight, and the Lord's holy day honorable, if you honor it by not going your own way or seeking your own pleasure or speaking idle words, then you will delight yourself in the Lord, and I will make you ride on the heights of the land and feed you with the heritage of your father Jacob (**Isaiah 58:1-14 BSB**).

I believe this passage from God through Isaiah is a promise over us today, a call to fasting. Perhaps you have never fasted a day in your life, you don't even know what or how to fast. I encourage you to read Lou's book on fasting and others like his; armor yourself with this spiritual weapon, for the days are dark. But God's promise is ever before us; as we move as one with this militant strategy of the Lord, He will interrupt the night, just as is promised in verses 8 and 9 (BSB):

Then your light will break forth like the dawn, and your healing will come quickly. Your righteousness will go before you, and the glory of the Lord will be your rear guard. Then you will call, and the Lord will answer; you will cry out, and He will say, "Here I am."

Daughter, you are called to be like a well-watered garden, and the Esther mantle is an anointing to rebuild the ancient ruins, to restore the age-old foundations, to repair the breach, and to restore the streets to dwell in. It's time to rend the heavens and break open God's promises over the earth in these last days.

NOTES

1. Strong's Hebrew Concordance #7167.

2. Strong's Greek Concordance #4977.

9

WAR AT THE TABLE

BIBLE READING: ESTHER 5-6

I had a dream last year where I saw Esther sitting at the banquet table with the king alongside her and Haman opposite her. In the dream, their feasting table was filled only with bread and red wine. Esther poured red wine into a gold chalice and handing it across the table, she gave it to Haman. Then she said to him, "Drink up." His eyes appeared happy and full of excitement, feeling honored by the queen. He took the chalice from Esther's hands, lifting it to his mouth and tipping his head back, he began to drink the red wine.

No sooner had the first drop entered his mouth, did something begin to happen. His face contorted and his eyes began to bulge. He was choking on the wine. Dropping the cup, it spilled all down his elegant clothing, staining all of it; then with his hands to his throat, he fell to the ground, falling at the feet of Esther, and he died. At that, I woke up. I knew immediately that the Holy Spirit was showing me that Esther's banquet table was a prophetic picture of Jesus's Passover table where the Blood of the Lamb would choke the spirit of Haman in our day.

TAKING THE BATTLE TO THE BLOOD

It is no secret that one of the callings God has placed upon my life has been to pray to see the end of abortion. Even with the victorious fall of Goliath—Roe v. Wade—there are still many battles ahead to see Goliath's brothers chased and annihilated from the nations. Six months on from the fall of Roe v. Wade, many will remember the fierce controversy following the Supreme Court's ruling. State governors in the United States were vowing to make their states "abortion sanctuaries" (such an oxymoron if ever there was one), while others were fighting back and outlawing abortion altogether in theirs.

Meanwhile, apostate pastors were declaring, "We are embarrassed by some of the rejoicing of other Christians at the fall of Roe." I have one statement for this kind of response, the apostate church of today would have mourned the death of Goliath in David's day. I'll move right along.

As though true Christians don't need more evidence that abortion is demonic, I'll never forget opening Instagram in January 2023 and discovering that a group called "the satanic temple" had just announced they would be opening a ritualistic abortion center in New Mexico, touting it as the "world's first religious abortion center." Attempting to come from the angle of a religious right, they wanted to make abortion become a "First Amendment" right of practice.

Initially, they were offering this as a late-term abortion clinic, and at first were declaring the opening of a physical location somewhere in New Mexico. The address was shrouded in secrecy, undisclosed to the public. What's more, as I researched a little deeper about their practices, I discovered that after leading a woman through a ritualistic abortion, they would complete the ritual of the baby's death by having the mother repeat the words, "By my body, by my blood, by my will, it is done." The moment I read those words, a righteous anger arose within me. I'm certain you see it too—the direct mockery of the words of Jesus on the night of the Passover before His crucifixion. These blasphemous words, coined by satan himself, reveal just how satanic abortion is. It is modern-day Baal worship, sacrificing the blood of innocent little ones for "self," as opposed to the atoning Blood of Jesus that was sacrificed for us.

When I read those words, I turned to Nate and said, "Someone has to do something." No sooner had this sentence come out of my mouth, I heard the Holy Spirit immediately reply, "Yes, and YOU are that someone!"

I smiled as I told Nate what I heard, to which he laughed, replying, "Yes, that sounds about right."

I asked the Holy Spirit, "What would You have me do?"

The very next day, we were on a family outing together in north Dallas, and as we were driving along a country road, out of nowhere, a tall, unusual-looking bird dashed across the road directly in front of us. Not close enough that we had to slow down, but within a near enough proximity that we were able to see it clearly. I had seen these birds before when we lived in Redding, California.

"I think that's a roadrunner," I said to Nate. The thought then came to my mind to look up what the state bird of New Mexico is. As I pulled up the search on my phone while Nate continued driving, the answer appeared that the state bird of New Mexico is the roadrunner. I turned to Nate again, "I think we're going to New Mexico." The Holy Spirit was confirming that He wanted us to plant our feet on the ground there to pray.

Over the coming days, the Holy Spirit began to unravel a prophetic act that He would require us to walk out. I knew we needed to invite people to come and pray with us somewhere in New Mexico, so I put out a call on Instagram and we had immediate responses. However, I was unsure of where to go, as I initially wanted to head to the physical location of the satanic temple and have a gathering of prayer directly there.

During my search for where to pray, I heard the Holy Spirit say, "No, I don't want you to go to the pits, you're going to take this battle to the heights."

That night I had a dream. I was standing alongside a river that was completely red like blood, and I saw a sign next to it that said, "Red River." I was drawing water out of it and taking communion from it.

Following that dream, Nate and I knew that this was about prayer and communion. Intrigued about the Red River sign, we opened a map to see if there might be something like this name in New Mexico. To our absolute amazement, there is indeed a river in New Mexico called Red River. What's more, there is also a town by the same name through which the Red River flows.

You must remember that we're Australians who haven't grown up in the United States. The only city I knew of in New Mexico was Albuquerque, and that was only because of a children's movie I loved as a child called *Psalty's Salvation Celebration*. Psalty the Singing Songbook and the children go on a gospel tour with the final stop being Albuquerque. That is all I knew of New Mexico. All to say, we knew the Holy Spirit was leading us, because we had no idea this town even existed.

When we updated on social media that we were planning on meeting in Red River, New Mexico, our friends reached out to us saying, "I think Red River may be located in the Blood of Christ Mountains." My jaw dropped. "Is there really such a place?" I asked. Sure enough, we opened the map once more and discovered that Red River was indeed located within the Sangre De Cristo Mountains. Again, we weren't even aware of this mountain range, which translates into English, "the Blood of Christ." I now understood in more depth why the Holy Spirit had initially said to me, "You're going to take this battle to the heights." We were taking the warfare to the Blood of the Lamb, to the table of communion. We were going to fight with the very weapon the enemy was mocking—the Blood of Jesus.

Still unsure of all the details of where exactly along this Red River we would meet, we asked the Holy Spirit for further confirmation. Nate and I opened a map once more and as we zoomed in to the little alpine town of Red River, we found a community center that backed directly onto the river itself. It was just as I had seen in my dream, where we took communion along the Red River. What's more, we discovered that right along the same street was an RV resort by the name of…Roadrunner.

Why does God work like this, you might ask? Proverbs 25:2 (CSB) says, *"It is the glory of God to conceal a matter and the glory of kings to investigate a matter* [search it out]." The Lord is longing for you to search out the matters of His heart, it's a relationship. I also believe the Lord really enjoys the fun of it; He loves to unveil

His secrets to us, and He delights in our searching and working with Him to bring His solutions to earth. I would also like to suggest, it is God's masterful strategy to conceal these plans in plain sight from the enemy. By partnering with Him and searching out the solutions of His heart, we overcome the enemy, right under satan's nose. We knew this was all confirmation.

That next morning, we woke up discussing our plans for making our way to New Mexico (in what would be just a few short weeks), and as we were discussing it, a roadrunner bird suddenly appeared in our backyard. It danced around, stared at us for a good while, then disappeared. I began pondering what this meant, beyond the fact that it is the state bird of New Mexico.

The infamous cartoon character, Roadrunner, came to my mind that I used to watch when I was younger, and I loved how the little roadrunner bird always outran the coyote. No matter what trap the coyote set before him, the roadrunner just happily continued his way, blissfully unaware of the threat against his life. It was the coyote that fell into his own traps and ended up beaten, battered, and bruised by the closing of the show. There is a line in the show's theme song that says, "That crazy coyote, when will he learn that he can never mow him (the roadrunner) down."

I believe the Holy Spirit was showing me, through this little interesting bird, that when we take the battle to the heights, the enemy cannot mow us down as we apply the Blood of Jesus. We're like the roadrunner, running constantly ahead of the enemy's traps; he can't catch us. We met on a crisp February afternoon, and the body of Christ in New Mexico packed out that little community hall; many had traveled miles upon miles to meet us there. Dear friends from Australia even sent one of their church hubs, located in New Mexico, to come and join us and lead us in worship. This truly felt like a gathering of the Body of Christ from all over, joining around the Blood of the Lamb. We spent hours in worship and prayer together, and then we walked outside. As we did, we immediately noticed a group of deer, we counted 12, that had gathered by the river and were drinking from the Red River.

Habakkuk 3:19 (BSB) immediately came to my mind: *"God, the Lord is my strength; He makes my feet like those of a deer; He makes me walk upon the heights!"* Just as the Holy Spirit had said, "You are taking this battle to the heights!" Then, as I had seen in my dream, hundreds of us gathered by the river. And as we stood in a circle and held high the cups representing the Blood of the Lamb over New Mexico, we lifted a battle cry against the satanic decree of bloodshed through abortion.

We took communion together, beholding the Lamb alongside the river of "blood." I know something shifted in the heavenly realm that day. It was later reported that the satanic temple shifted their supposed physical clinic to a virtual one, limiting their ability to perform all trimester abortions. I firmly believe that this one little gathering put an end to their intended late-term abortion clinic. They no longer have the physical "temple" of ritualistic abortions they had lauded to offer. Though we are still waging war against this principality, I am confident that we will continue to see the fruit of the full victory as we run ahead, like the roadrunner, with communion in the days and months to come.

I share this story with you, because I believe the Holy Spirit is bringing to our attention our greatest weapon in this hour, which is and always has been the Blood of Jesus. I believe that the body of Christ has not realized the full potential of what the river of His

Blood is capable of, and we have treated the partaking of communion as a religious tradition rather than wielding it as the weapon that it truly is.

If the enemy can mock it so openly, there is a reason he is doing so—mockery reveals his deep contempt for what the Blood of Jesus does to him. Dare I say that in the years past, satan has understood the value of the Blood of Jesus better than the ecclesia, the church, and he has attempted to lull us into thinking this is nothing more than an act of remembrance. Satan knows the power of the Blood can disarm his own powers, so he has cleverly mocks or dulls our understanding of it. Why else would he be leading mothers to abort their children and then, in an open act of extreme rebellion against Jesus, have them declare a direct insult of Christ's words about communion—sacrificing the broken body of their babies unto themselves, as opposed to receiving the broken body of Jesus for their sins.

Luke 22:19-20 (NIV) says, *"And he took bread, gave thanks and broke it, and gave it to them, saying, "This is my body given for you; do this in remembrance of me. In the same way, after the supper he took the cup, saying, "This cup is the new covenant in my blood, which is poured out for you."*

I saw a video recently of a hawk that had caught a snake. The hawk had its talons on the head of the snake, and it seemed as though the hawk was the victor with its next meal at the ready. However, in one split second, the snake lifted its tail behind the hawk, and began to curl its tail around the head of the hawk. Within mere seconds, the hawk was strangled to death, falling backward under the pinning strength of the snake and it died.

An eagle, on the other hand, knows that to devour a snake, it cannot easily win the battle on the ground. The eagle instead, grabs the head of the snake and lifts it off the ground, where the snake loses its power and balance. The snake will try to fight, but without the ground, it's powerless. The eagle wins the battle in the heights.

In the same way, we are about to witness how Esther, too, grabbed the head of the snake and carried it to the heights, slamming its head upon the table—the table of communion.

ESTHER WARS AT THE TABLE

In this chapter's reading of Scripture, you would have read the entirety of Esther chapter 5. I want to read parts of Esther 5 with you as we revisit the dream I shared earlier on, and break down the profound and integral elements in this section of Esther's story.

> *On the third day Esther put on her royal robes and stood in the inner court of the palace, in front of the king's hall. The king was sitting on his royal throne in the hall, facing the entrance. When he saw Queen Esther standing in the court, he was pleased with her and held out to her the gold scepter that was in his hand. So Esther approached and touched the tip of the scepter* (**Esther 5:1-2 NIV**).

Every detail of Esther's actions here are weighty with prophetic allegory. Esther finished her fast on the third day, then she put on her royal robes in preparation of going before the king. In the

Hebrew language, the number three represents resurrection (overcoming death), revelation, strength and firstfruits. (Make a mental note of the points of resurrection and firstfruits particularly, for this will come into play later on.)

Esther was walking into the revelation that the Lord had set before her. By the strength of the Father (remember, her father's name, Abihail, means "father of strength), she was about to see the fruit of her trust in the Lord. What's more, the Hebrew word used here to describe her royal robes is the word *malkuth,* which means "royal power."[1] I love that! Esther put on her royal power, and you too, daughter, can put on supernatural royal power and strength when you are walking in the mantle of Esther.

I can just see it now, the moment Esther put on those royal robes, or rather royal power, a supernatural courage rested upon her. Maybe she didn't feel it prior to that moment, but as we read, she grows in strength as the verses move on, and I wholeheartedly believe it was the divine courage of the Father that was mantling her. Imagine knowing, *"this day I could die,"* but still, she walked to the boundary of her potential death, the inner courtyard.

Now this I find fascinating. The inner courtyard in Scripture represents the inner place of the tabernacle, and today it speaks of our own hearts being the inner courtyard of the sanctuary of the Holy Spirit. Esther had to die to herself and surrender to the call.

Lest I lose you here, as I could share an entire chapter on the tabernacle alone, I find it amazing, that this is where Esther receives favor in the eyes of the king. He sees her in the inner courtyard; and rather than being filled with rage that she has come unannounced, Scripture tells us, *"she gained favor in his eyes."* Could this be speaking, perhaps, in a parabolic way of how we too find favor with our King when we leave our old selves behind and pursue Him with our lives laid down in the inner courtyard of our hearts? Do you recall Kim Clement's prophecy about Esther, with the big, beautiful eyes? What I find significant here is that the king's eyes are drawn to hers.

The king extends his gold scepter, which represents authority and strength, and is the Hebrew word *shebet*,[2] which describes it as a mark of authority. In other words, the king extended his authority to her, and by touching it, she was receiving his governmental dominion. Upon receiving this authority Esther invites the king and Haman to the table.

I want to pause on this thought for just a moment. It is by the authority of the king that Esther invites the battle to the table. It is an unseen move by Haman, he is expecting a feast, but he is about to choke on the Lamb. How many battles have you been trying to fight in your own strength today? Down on the ground, you've been warring like that hawk, when instead the Father is whispering, "Hey, daughter, you have My authority, carry him to the heights, bring him to the table."

Esther then says, *"If it pleases the king,"* she says, *"may the king and Haman come today to the banquet I have prepared for them"* (Esther 5:4 CSB). As we read later in this text, Haman was pleasantly surprised at this request; he found it to be a great honor to be invited to the table. Interesting. God was moving him into position where the queen was about to become the threat, and by inviting him to the table, Esther was carrying him to the heights—above the noise of his declarations, above the chaos of the battle. Remember, the feast here, I believe, is a prophetic picture of the table of communion—and little did Haman know he was about to choke on the prophetic picture of the Blood of the Lamb.

I'm reminded of this verse from David's Psalm 23:5 (CSB), *"You prepare a table before me in the presence of my enemies; you anoint my head with oil; my cup overflows."* Isn't it striking that oil is mentioned in this verse; think of the alabaster jar of oil we talked about. Esther's preparation of oil and perfumes led her to this moment, she was anointed for this *kairos.* Now her cup overflows, which can also point to the cup of the Lamb. In Esther 5:6 (CSB), we read, *"While drinking the wine, the king asked Esther* [again], *'Whatever you ask will be given to you....'"* This is a critical moment. The king is drinking the wine, yet another foreshadow of the Blood of Jesus.

While the king is drinking the wine, he once more extends his authority to Esther, asking her in essence, "Ask of me, and I will give you whatever you want." Once more, this is pointing to the power of our ask. When we take communion, we are not just remembering a symbol of what Jesus did, we are asking Him to release the same potent power of His Blood that cut the veil of the temple in two, we are asking Him to release His New Covenant into our lives and to spill His Blood over into the issues of our day—we are making a demand on the wonder-working power of the Cross.

Upon the king's request, Esther uses her petition wisely. Rather than immediately exposing Haman in the moment, she asks for another banquet the following evening. Have you ever wondered why she delays and repeats the banquet a second time? I know I certainly have. I've often questioned, "Was she afraid? Is that why she delayed a day, so she could gain more courage?" My curiosity led me to research why, and let me just say that what I discovered made me scream out loud in amazement.

I don't believe that Esther delayed out of fear. I can now say with confidence that there was indeed a strategic timing in play with her second banquet. Do you recall at the beginning of this book how I mentioned the significance of the word *time*? How it speaks into both *chronos* and *kairos*. As a Jewish woman, Esther would have known the significance of the days and times, so my firm belief is that she knew exactly what she was doing.

Before I share my findings with you, which to be honest I can't contain without excitement, I must first show you what took place the night of the first banquet and the following day before the second banquet.

KAIROS IN MOTION

Haman was being moved into a supernatural collision of God's *kairos* timing converging into this *chronos* moment. The night following the first banquet, we read in Esther 5:9-14 (CSB):

> *Haman left full of joy and in good spirits. But when Haman saw Mordecai at the King's Gate, and Morde-cai didn't rise or tremble in fear at his presence, Haman was filled with rage toward Mordecai. Yet Haman controlled himself and went home. He sent for his friends and his wife Zeresh to join him. Then Haman described for them his glorious wealth and his many sons. He told them all how the king had honored him and promoted*

*him in rank over the other officials and the royal staff.
"What's more," Haman added, "Queen Esther invited
no one but me to join the king at the banquet she had
prepared. I am invited again tomorrow to join her with
the king. Still, none of this satisfies me since I see Mordecai the Jew sitting at the King's Gate all the time." His
wife Zeresh and all his friends told him, "Have them
build a gallows seventy-five feet tall. Ask the king in
the morning to hang Mordecai on it. Then go to the
banquet with the king and enjoy yourself." The advice
pleased Haman, so he had the gallows constructed.*

In this text alone, we see the principality of Haman in full operation. He reveals his pride in the exaltation of himself to his friends,
boasts about his high position, and exposes himself through his
utter contempt and hatred of Mordecai (who we now know is a
picture of Jesus). I love in these verses how it emphasizes Mordecai's utter resolve to refuse to bow before him. In a comparable
story told in Matthew 4:1-11, we find satan attempting to force
Jesus to bow to him through bribery. Of course, Jesus refused to do
so. Mordecai, too, watches Haman pass him by, and he did not rise
to him or tremble in fear at his presence, despite knowing the edict
of death that Haman had released upon him. Mordecai stood firm,
knowing that God alone was His rescue.

Another key person in the Scriptures from Esther 5, is Haman's
wife, Zeresh. We read of her in the previous chapter, and now it
is time to pay attention to her because she plays a key role with
the principality of Haman. In Vashti's fall, we see Haman rise,
and alongside Haman is his wife, Zeresh. This is where things get
interesting. If you recall, Vashti's name also meant "daughter of

Ishtar." So with Vashti's removal, what happens to Ishtar? Was she too removed from her high place? No. We find her hiding behind Zeresh whose name means "golden star of adoration." Ishtar too, means golden star. Notice Zeresh is a mother, and Ishtar as well is named "mother goddess." Ishtar works through those who give her power.

Of course, we know that Esther's Persian name means simply "star." Zeresh is Ishtar, the counterfeit of Esther. In these last days, we will see both the true daughters arising, carrying the pure mantle of Esther that shines the true morning star of Jesus, and we will also see the counterfeits, the Zereshes who are the dim representatives of the counterfeit "morning star" of Ishtar/satan. It's easy to spot Zeresh/Ishtar today; she is in opposition to everything that is godly and true. She denies the Lord and helps to set traps for those who are walking in righteousness. Notice it is Zeresh, along with Haman's friends, who conspire the idea of building a 75-foot-tall gallows and demand Mordecai's immediate death.

Today, Zeresh demands death and cancellation to anyone who opposes her and her husband—the principality of Haman. If you refuse to bow to their intimidation, she screams, "Death! Cancel their voices!" Take note of the vicious modern rise of the recent waves of feminism; theirs is the voice of Zeresh/Ishtar.

However, Zeresh, too, was being played right into a *kairos* of God. Her own suggestion to build the gallows was a snare of the Lord set by her own words. The word for *gallows* in Hebrew is *ets*.[3] It simply means "a tree." It's the same word used to describe the Cross. Given that Haman was familiar with Jewish custom, it's highly probable that he and his wife were accustomed with the

Jewish law of hanging a man on a tree. Deuteronomy 21:23 (CSB) says, *"...anyone who is hung on a **tree** is under God's curse...."* In effect, they wanted to humiliate Mordecai as a *firstfruits* of the slaughter to come and declare him as cursed by God on this tree. Do you see the parallel to Jesus here? This plan of Zeresh's only furthermore solidifies Mordecai as a foreshadow of Jesus. Just wait though, it gets much deeper.

HAMAN CHOKES ON THE BLOOD

Haman wakes up the following morning after the first banquet, and as we studied in the previous chapter, he is led through, might I say, quite a hilarious day of humiliation prior to the second banquet that evening. His plans to execute Mordecai had not only failed, but failed miserably, and he was led through a torturous day of honoring the man he despised so vehemently.

This then leads us to Esther chapter 7—Haman's execution, which we will study in greater detail in the next chapter. However, I want to lead you back to the questions I asked earlier, "Why did Esther delay a day? Why did she ask for a second banquet?" Now I reveal to you why. The day of the second banquet and Haman's imminent execution, fell upon the 17th day of the Hebrew month of Nissan. Esther delayed for a profound reason. I searched a multitude of Hebraic historical records, high and low, and found unanimous confirmation in all of them. The following list is a historical record of what took place in biblical history on Nissan 17.

1. Noah's Ark finds rest upon the peak of Mount Ararat (Genesis 8:4).

2. The Hebrews enter Egypt, 430 years to the day before their deliverance would come to pass (Exodus 12:40-41).

3. Moses leads the Israelites through the parting of the Red Sea (Exodus 3:18, 5:3).

4. Israel enters and eats the *firstfruits* of the Promised Land (Joshua 5:10-12).

5. The temple is cleansed by Hezekiah (2 Chronicles 29:1-28).

Esther knew. The Red Sea had parted that very day, it was a day of deliverance for the Jewish people, and the day that Pharoah and his armies were crushed under the waters of the Red Sea. Prophetically speaking, the Israelites, too, had led Pharaoh to the table of the blood, and Pharaoh and his army also choked in the sea of blood. Esther was prophetically aligning herself to the timing of the Lord; and just as I had dreamed of her, in no less words, she made Haman "drink up." Then his death would mark another date on this significant day of Nissan 17: Haman is hung and Queen Esther is victorious in saving the Jews from annihilation (Esther 3:12, 5:1).

However, that is not all. The final and most powerful event that would later occur on this exact same day, Nissan 17, some 440 years later, would be the most cataclysmic event of all history: Jesus Christ, the Messiah was resurrected from the dead. To say I screamed when I saw that final point would be an understatement.

There is some argument over the dates; however, from my findings it is almost unanimous among scholars that Jesus was indeed raised from the dead on Nissan 17, the same day historically, that Haman was hung.

This points to the bigger picture, that Haman was a prophetic foreshadow of Jesus's ultimate victory over satan through the Cross. Haman hangs on a tree the same day that Jesus is raised from death on a tree, hundreds of years later. Haman choked on the blood. Jesus is hidden throughout the book of Esther, and the overarching theme is consistent: the Blood of the Lamb is where we find our victory over every demon principality today. If we look at the symbolism of each of the historical events that took place on Nissan 17, leading up to Haman's hanging, you will find it confirmed once again:

1. Noah's ark represents our salvation and purification from sin; the ark sealed as the floodwaters cover the earth points to the promise of the New Covenant that would be found in Jesus (1 Peter 3:18-22).

2. The Hebrews taken into slavery represents our slavery to sin, but God's promise of deliverance was coming (Romans 8:15 Galatians 5:1).

3. The parting of the Red Sea (and the Passover) points to Jesus; His blood is the "red sea" we walk through for our deliverance (1 Corinthians 10:1-4).

4. The Israelites eating the firstfruits (remember this from earlier?), pointing to Jesus once more as the firstfruits of our salvation (1 Corinthians 15:20).

5. The cleansing of the temple aims at the coming cleansing that Jesus would do through His body for ours. It was a prophetic picture of our temple—body, soul, and spirit—being purified by His blood (Luke 19:45-48).

6. Haman's death is a picture of the complete victory over satan through the work of the Cross. Jesus would hang upon the cursed tree in our place, and make a spectacle of Haman (Colossians 2:15).

We can conclude then that Esther did not delay for fear or trepidation, she was moving Haman right into the delivering hand of the Lord. She became the shining star, declaring His glory—in complete annihilation of the golden star, the idol of Zeresh/Ishtar. She brought Haman to the table and, prophetically speaking, made him choke on the Blood of the Lamb.

COMMUNION, OUR WEAPON OF WARFARE

I am often asked, "What is your greatest piece of advice for spiritual warfare?" My answer is always, "Communion." I'm usually met with a stunned look, as many are expecting an answer such as, "Pray for five days straight" or "Pray in tongues" or "Spend three hours in worship." While all those elements are great, I feel we are all too often looking for a formula, a list of ingredients, a ten-step plan, when we have already been given the greatest weapon there possibly is—the body and Blood of Jesus.

Imagine, if instead of trying to defeat the enemy through our own actions by wrestling with him in ground warfare, that we brought him up to the heights and sat him at the table of the Lord where he loses his strength and stamina. Where God has prepared a table before us in the presence of our enemies. We get to feast on the Lamb instead of screaming and shouting and wearing ourselves out—and yes, there is a time and place for shouting. Instead, our warfare becomes a feast in the place of a battle. We declare the victory of the Blood of the Lamb. We give voice to the testimony of His Blood that still speaks today—a better word over darkness and evil (Hebrews 12:24).

What if we discovered that we have the ability to walk through impossibilities as the Israelites walked through the Red Sea, by the power of His Blood? What if we understood that our weapon is a banquet of His body and Blood, and we carry Haman to the table? What if we truly grasped the understanding in our day that every battle we face is won by the sprinkled Blood of the atoning, spotless Lamb? How many more victories would we see, if together, the body of Christ collectively stopped playing games and instead started engaging in true warfare by lifting the body of the Lamb and declaring His victory over the principalities of Haman in our day?

What if this is what Revelation 12:11 (KJV) is speaking of: *"They overcame him by the blood of the Lamb, and by the word of their testimony...."* What if this is the key, in these last days, that we must grasp, take a hold of, and use?

Can I propose to you that this isn't a "What if" time in history—but a "What is!" *It is* the declaration, the prevailing reminder, the remembrance and the *testimony* of what Jesus did on the Cross that disarms, disengages, and disempowers every lying spirit and principality we are facing in our day. It is the power of the Cross that causes Haman to choke and fall. I am convinced that the greatest revelation of the mantle of Esther is the mantle of the finished work of the Cross. That crazy enemy, when will he learn, he can never mow Jesus down.

Bring the enemy to the table of the Blood—and watch his powers fall.

NOTES

1. Strong's Hebrew Concordance #4438.

2. Strong's Hebrew Concordance #7626.

3. Strong's Hebrew Concordance #6086.

PART FOUR

the
ESTHER
Victory

ATONEMENT

BIBLE READING: ESTHER 7

I am no expert when it comes to playing chess, but I am familiar with the basic rules of play, and I especially love a good checkmate. Checkmate occurs when the king is trapped in a position of threat or check and the opposing queen takes a certain position opposite him, making it impossible for him to move. Thus the king is checkmated and the game is over, with the win going to the queen. This is precisely what God is doing through the mantle of Esther. Once Esther is crowned in chapter 3, she is no longer referred to as simply Esther, her name takes on the new form of Queen Esther.

I want you to observe the hand of the Lord moving this queen in divine strategies against the demonic prince, the enemy game piece of Haman. What satan does not see in our day today are the unexpected moves God is making through His daughters, mantled with the robes of Queen Esther. The Lord is positioning you in ways the enemy cannot fathom; and before satan can anticipate it, God will have moved His queens into positions of great threat for the principality of Ishtar/Haman—and it will be game over for him. Checkmate.

THE PUR

We're going to revisit Esther chapter 3 again, because I want to show you that before Esther and Mordecai even knew what Haman was up to, God was already at work, moving strategically, setting him up for a checkmate. Esther 3:7 (CSB) tells us, *"In the first month, the month of Nisan, in King Ahasuerus's twelfth year, the pur—that is, the lot—was cast before Haman for each day in each month, and it fell on the twelfth month, the month Adar."* Let's pause on this verse.

First, you may ask, what is *pur*, or casting lots? It sounds like a modern-day lottery, and while the words are connected, this ancient biblical practice was not a form of trying to win money; rather, it was an effort to hear the voice of God for any given situation. Casting lots is mentioned throughout the Old Testament and some in the New, before the release of the Holy Spirit in Acts. This practice is no longer needed in any capacity because we now have the indwelling of the Holy Spirit. Whereas in the Old Testament, they didn't have access to the presence of God, or His voice, the way we do today. So it was customary, and even supported by God, for people to cast lots to hopefully hear where He was leading them on a matter. I also want to emphasize that this was in no way like the divination of a Ouija board where people call on the names of the dead. No, this was much different. This was seeking out the voice of God for critical decisions that needed to be made.

It's ironic here that we find Haman doing such a thing. Why would he be seeking the voice of God, you may ask? As with anything pertaining to the Lord, you will always find the enemy operating in a form of direct mockery and counterfeit. Gambling also comes from this concept; however, it too is a counterfeit of what casting lots was in its original form, which was to hear the voice of God.

We find the last mention of casting lots in the New Testament, in Acts 1:26, where the disciples cast lots to replace Judas. Following this occasion, the gift of the Holy Spirit is released upon the disciples and the need to hear His voice through this ancient practice of lots, dies. His voice now dwells among us and within us.

Moving on.

The Hebrew word *pur* literally means "lots." But there are some considerations where it may also mean "to break into pieces or crumbs." Ironically, that's the very plan Haman intended—he wanted to break God's people into pieces. The reason for this meaning is because shards of broken pottery were often used to "cast the lots" by writing the names or places of things in question on these shards, then throwing them on the ground and asking God to reveal the answer. Their answer would be found in whichever piece landed in a certain way.

The practice of casting lots, however, was not held by Israel alone, the ancient Greeks and Persians also cast lots, and whether they acquired this practice from Israel or not, I'm unsure. The point is, Haman was playing right into God's hands, he thought he was casting lots to break the Jews into pieces, but he would be the one broken into crumbs, for God had another plan. Haman was walking right into the trap set before him, from the very moment he set his mind against Mordecai and God's people.

Esther 9:24-26 (BSB) reads:

> *For Haman son of Hammedatha, the Agagite, the enemy of all the Jews, had plotted against the Jews to destroy them and had cast the Pur (that is, the lot) to crush and destroy them. But when it came before the king, he commanded by letter that the wicked scheme which Haman had devised against the Jews should come back upon his own head, and that he and his sons should be hanged on the gallows. Therefore these days are called Purim, from the word Pur.*

This Scripture passage is a "checkmate." The very method that Haman had used to scheme against the Jews came back upon his own head. Let's find out how. The Holy Spirit led me to go back through Scripture and study where the first mention of "lots" was recorded in the Bible. This might seem like a trivial piece to the story of Esther; however, Haman's casting of the lot was mentioned twice in the book of Esther, and to this day, the Jewish festival of Purim that celebrates Esther's and Mordecai's victory is in fact, named after the *pur*. There is a principle when studying Scripture called the principle of first mention. What does that mean? The first mention of a word or concept often establishes a precedent or pattern that then gives you the context for the biblical concept. You will often find this same precedent is repeated throughout other Scriptures in the Bible following the first mention.

So with that in mind, I searched to find where this first mention occurs for the "lot." What I found astounded me, confirming that

God was working behind the scenes to set Haman in a position where the very threat he was to the Jewish people, became the very threat that took his life.

Another Hebraic word used for *lot* is *goral* and it means "destiny or fate." The first mention of *goral,* or the casting of lots, is found in Leviticus 16:8 where the Day of Atonement is laid out before Moses and Aaron.

> *After Aaron* **casts lots** *for the two goats,* **one lot** *for the Lord and the other for an uninhabitable place, he is to present the goat* **chosen by lot** *for the Lord and sacrifice it as a sin offering. But the goat* **chosen by lot** *for an uninhabitable place is to be presented alive before the Lord to make atonement with it by sending it into the wilderness for an uninhabitable place* (**Leviticus 16:8-10 CSB**).

I know this is a rabbit trail of sorts, but bear with me while we break this down together, because what you are going to see is the snare that has been set for Haman through his own schemes.

The Day of Atonement is the highest day of the year, the day that in retrospect of the New Covenant, is a foreshadow of the atoning work of Jesus Christ, *Yeshua Hamashiach.* Every detail laid out in Leviticus 16 points to Jesus, and the mere fact that the lot was mentioned here is yet another profound symbolism of the coming work of the Cross. What's more, it points to the destiny of Haman and God's people. Haman cast lots or fate and destiny for himself.

The two goats mentioned in Leviticus 16:8 where the lot is cast for them are once more profound symbolism for Jesus and the checkmate that Haman would fall into. The two goats are a full picture of Christ's atoning work on the Cross. One goat is presented to the Lord as a sin offering, where the sins of the people are forgiven through its blood, and the other is to be presented alive before the Lord to make atonement for the sins of the people, then the goat was sent out into the wilderness into an uninhabitable place so their sins would be forgotten.

I want to focus for a moment on the scapegoat, the one sent into the wilderness, so we can uncover why this is connected to Haman through the casting of lots.

Leviticus 16:20-22 (CSB) says:

> *When he has finished making atonement for the most holy place, the tent of meeting, and the altar, he is to present the live male goat. Aaron will lay both his hands on the head of the live goat and confess over it all the Israelite's iniquities and rebellious acts—all their sins. He is to put them on the goat's head and send it away into the wilderness by the man appointed for the task. The goat will carry all their iniquities into a desolate land, and the man will release it there.*

I encourage you to focus your attention on the *"man appointed for the task."* I believe a more accurate translation of this verse reads, *"...send it away into the wilderness by the hand of a man appointed for the task"* (Leviticus 16:21 BSB). The word *appointed* is the Hebrew word *itti,* which means "timely and ready." You may remember at the beginning of this book, in Chapter 1, how I mentioned the *kairos* and *chronos* collision of *"for such a time as this!"* This verse speaking of the man carrying away the scapegoat speaks of how there is a man appointed for the task (Hint: it's also Jesus) who will carry away the scapegoat at the right time. I believe this prophetically points to Haman being carried away; and once again, speaking to our own day, there is coming a time of the carrying away of the "scapegoat."

Now, I encourage you to see this clearly. The two goats are prophetic of Jesus: one is the atoning goat for the temple, the other is an atoning goat for our sins. They point to the cleansing Blood of Jesus where our sins are forgiven and then forgotten. However, there's one other detail that stands out to me in this profound parallel. Not explicitly mentioned in this verse, but found within Hebraic tradition, is that the goat was not left to wander alone and starve to death in the wilderness, for fear that it might find its way back into the camp, bringing with it the sin upon its head that was meant to be forgotten. The scapegoat was instead led by the appointed man, to the edge of a high cliff where it was thrown off. This goat being the atoning goat, suffered a more horrific death than its counterpart, because as recorded by many scholars, it was traditional for the goat to be led to a specific cliff that had protruding rocks jutting out all the way to the ground. The scapegoat would have been cut and torn to pieces on the way down—which leads us back to the "lot," which can mean "to break into pieces."

The scapegoat is a profound picture of the Lamb that was slain, cut to pieces; and it is additionally the picture of the sins that entangle us and the snares of the enemy that would bind us. It is simultaneously a picture of the Man being Jesus Himself, leading the enemy over the cliff, breaking him into pieces—instead of us. Another piece of God's poetic tapestry can be weaved into this story right here. Remember the name meanings of Mordecai and his forefathers: He that is renowned and famous, will be crushed and oppressed for he will enlighten and expose the snare (refer to Chapter 6).

Do you see the incredible design in Scripture here? Where Haman was attempting to exploit the lot—originally used to hear the voice of God in the Old Testament—he ended up falling into the trap set before him. The snare he had set, became the very snare he fell into. God used Mordecai—a foreshadow of Jesus—to expose the snare. Haman attempted to determine a favorable day for his snare to crush God's people, and instead he was met with his own fate and destiny. I believe Haman is the picture of the scapegoat—he was cast out into the wilderness and pushed down into the trap of his own devices, breaking him and his ancestry into pieces. Checkmate.

DOUBLE, TRIPLE CHECKMATE

Going back to Esther 3:7 (CSB) again, there is another important detail I must show you. It says, *"in the first month, the month of Nisan...the pur—that is, the lot—was cast before Haman...."* This is significant. Haman was setting up his plans for the annihilation of Jews during the month of *Nisan*. Why is Nisan important? Because Nisan is when Passover occurs. Here we have a second picture of the atoning Blood of the Lamb sitting in the foreshadows of Haman's plans. Haman was building his schemes upon the atoning Blood, without even realizing it.

The whole story of Passover signifies when God delivered His people out of the hands of Pharoah (Exodus 12). In the last and final plague that came upon Egypt, the firstborn sons died. But not the Israelites' firstborn, for they had been instructed to brush the blood of a spotless lamb upon their doorways. When the angel of death passed through Egypt, it passed over every home where the blood was on the doorposts, thus releasing them from the grip of Pharaoh. The Israelites were led forth to freedom, through the Red Sea (again, which speaks of the Blood of the Lamb.)

Unbeknown to Haman, he was casting lots during the month of the Passover, playing once more, right into God's hands just as Pharoah did. What's more, Jesus was later crucified on Passover, He became our Passover Lamb. Haman was put to death on the same day that the Israelites passed through the Red Sea, the same day that Jesus would later rise from the dead, Nisan 17.

I find it remarkable that there are those who say Jesus is not mentioned in the book of Esther, when in fact He is written about, though concealed, throughout the book. Today, where the principality of Haman/Ishtar is attempting to annihilate generations through violence, through ideas and ideologies, through the destruction of God's design in male and female, families, and even through violence of war and nations rising against nations, the blinded enemy cannot see that he too will fall upon the Blood of the Passover Lamb—*checkmate!*

Before problems ever raise their heads, God was already at work on our behalf. He sent His Son to die as the spotless Lamb upon the Cross, so that we can stand in the doorways of invisibility by His Blood. Our greatest weapon in this hour is the Blood of Jesus covering the doorways of our homes, our families, our cities, and our nations. The enemy is walking right into the trap set before him.

Furthermore, when those lots were cast before Haman, they fell on the twelfth month, the month of Adar. The Hebrew month of Adar comes from the word *adir,* which means "great, mighty and powerful, majestic and noble." It was also said among the Israelites, "When Adar enters, joy increases." This too, is speaking of the strength of *our King, Jesus.* It is *by Him and through Him* that we have our joy and our victory. This reminds me of the verse from Zechariah 4:6 (NIV), *"So he said to me, "This is the word of the Lord to Zerubbabel: 'Not by might nor by power, but by my Spirit,' says the Lord Almighty."* This is not a battle that will be won by physical weapons, but by the weapon of the Blood of Jesus. By His strength we will overcome the principality of Haman/Ishtar and watch him fall by his own sword. What was meant to be a time of great mourning, pain, and death, will turn into a time of outrageous joy and triumph, just as it did for Queen Esther and Mordecai. Haman was played right into his own demise—*checkmate!*

You might be asking, how can I walk this out practically? How can I pray into this and partner my faith with the Blood of Jesus for my children and their futures?

THE WEAPON OF COMMUNION

I recently had a dream where I saw a circle of modern-day prophets sitting at a table. They were strategizing about the battles we are currently facing, and on the table they each had their own books and strategies laid out. In the dream, I came and swiped everything off the table, and laid down the elements of communion as

I declared, "This is our weapon." Many on the table grew angry at me, with one woman shouting, "How dare you remove my book and my strategies. Do you know who I am?" At that, my friend Lou Engle appeared in the dream, he stood to my defense and shouted over their anger, "This is the ONLY weapon we need in this hour. It is the body and Blood of Jesus."

I believe we are going to see the fall of many who are only interested in advancing their own interests and platforms in this hour. Those who only care about their individual desires will be like the foolish virgins of the New Testament. Only those who desire to lift up the body and Blood of Jesus will walk in the true mantle of Esther, for this mantle requires purity and surrender.

You may be asking, "How do I wield the weapon of communion?" The answer is, daily. Take communion with your children and your family. Teach your children to remember the Blood of Jesus, and how to behold the Lamb. I believe this is what points back to the myrtle upon the booths—it is the mantle of Esther, carrying the atoning Blood of the Lamb into every home. Through this, the power of Ishtar and Haman are broken into pieces. Where Ishtar has pursued the home, God is restoring the home—and it comes through the Blood of the Lamb.

I believe you are going to see your marriage restored as you behold the Lamb. Your prodigals will return. Do you have children trapped under the spell of Ishtar right now? Have they believed the lies of transformation through lgbtq and sexuality? Take communion over them. Lift up the weapon of the body of Jesus and declare each time, "TELESTAI! IT IS FINISHED!" Let the enemy know his power has been broken over you, your family, your children, and your grandchildren. Declare the victory over your city, state, and nation—behold the Lamb.

THE POWER OF ASK

God wrote these incredible details into the story of Esther so we can see in our day the powerful weapon in our hands to strike down and annihilate the enemy we are facing in every realm of culture. We don't need to cast lots, we have the Blood of the Lamb written into our stories, and all we need to do is wield it. There is, however, another element of the Blood; and to find it, we need to read Esther 7:1-3 (CSB):

> The king and Haman came to feast with Esther the queen. Once again, on the second day while drinking wine, the king asked Esther, "Queen Esther, whatever you ask will be given to you. Whatever you seek, even to half the kingdom, will be done." Queen Esther answered, "If I have found favor with you, Your Majesty, and if the king is pleased, spare my life; this is my request. And spare my people; this is my desire."

There is an interesting play on King Ahasuerus's words here, which can be compared in likeness to the words Jesus spoken in Matthew 7:7-8 (CSB): "Ask, and it will be given to you. Seek, and you will find. Knock, and the door will be opened to you. For everyone who asks receives, and the who seeks finds, and to the one who knocks, the door will be opened."

The Greek word for *ask* is *aiteó,* and it means to "request, make petition for, demand." We can see the parallel here, where Esther makes a request to the king. The Hebrew word used for *request* in Esther's context is *baqash,* and it similarly means "to demand, to seek, desire and hold." What's the importance of this? All too often it is easy to feel overwhelmed at the prevailing pressures and evils of the world around us. We look at the troubles of our own lives, and then the culture in which we live, and it can be easy to want to bury our head in the sand and do nothing, say nothing. It is crucial that we learn to raise our voices and *ask* the Lord. We need to *seek* Him out and make a *demand* upon the Blood of Jesus to intervene on our behalf. If Esther had never spoken up at the right time, her life and the lives of her people would have been destroyed. We have to ask.

THE POWER OF THE TESTIMONY

Revisiting Esther's moment of courage with the king, we find that immediately after Esther reveals the plot against her and her people, the king inquires, *"Who is this, and where is the one who would devise such a scheme?"* (Esther 7:5 CSB). (There's that word *scheme* again.)

Notice upon Esther's testimony, Haman's scheme is uncovered and exposed! It is *the word of our testimony* that puts the Blood of Jesus to work. I've mentioned this verse before, but it's imperative I mention it once more here, as it is the VERY foundation of our victory. Revelation 12:11 (BSB) says, *"They have conquered him by the blood of the Lamb and by the word of their testimony. And they did not love their lives so as to shy away from death."*

There is a reason that the enemy, this principality of Haman, uses noise as one of his schemes. The noise of chaos and destruction. The noise of newsfeeds and comments, intimidation through noise. When there is so much noise, we want quiet, and we end up becoming quiet ourselves. However, it is the antidote of the voice of Esther—the word of her testimony—that silenced the accuser.

This is why, when it comes to issues such as abortion, I encourage women who have had abortions and found their redemption in Jesus to SHOUT their testimonies. Let it be heard in the streets, let it be heard from the high places—your testimony *moves* the Blood of Jesus. It activates and speaks in the spiritual realm that causes the enemy to tremble.

Hebrews 12:24 from the Amplified Bible says it like this:

> *And to Jesus, the Mediator of a new covenant [uniting God and man], and to the sprinkled blood, which speaks [of mercy], a better and nobler and more gracious message than the blood of Abel [which cried out for vengeance].*

Several years ago, late-term abortion legislation had just been introduced to my home state of Queensland, Australia. Legislation that, like Haman's legislation, was so evil and vile, giving the right for a woman to abort her baby right up until the moment of birth for any reason, even allowing, hidden in the legislation through cleverly crafted words, a buffer of up to three days post birth. If the mother decided she didn't want her baby once born, she could have that baby legally discarded.

I only wish I was exaggerating this horrible proposal to you, but sadly I'm not. What's more, written into this legislation was a safe-zone initiative for abortion clinics, that would outlaw anyone who wanted to pray outside of an abortion mill, within up to 100 meters (approximately 328 feet). This proposed legislation would imprison for two weeks anyone violating this safe-zone by praying within the set area. The enemy understood the power of prayer and devised to outlaw anyone praying in front of these murder mills. Statistically, 1 out of 3 women who see someone praying in front of an abortion mill will turn around and cancel their appointments.

At the time, I was involved with a pro-life group helping to raise awareness in churches and pastors in the region; we were trying to encourage them to engage in the battle, all to very little avail. We were ignored by 95 percent of the churches and pastors we reached out to, and told repetitively, "We don't like to engage in politics." So a small group of us, facing a seemingly impossible giant within our government, would go and pray during the parliamentary hearings. Not more than 20 of us showed up to stop this evil.

I'll never forget it. The feeling of overwhelming darkness; it was heavy in the room as they debated. We had to silently sit in the gallery, not allowed to make a noise or uproar at what we were hearing—and all I wanted to do was scream in opposition to the ghastly statements and lies I heard spew out of the mouths of demon-possessed politicians. I could strongly sense that I was witnessing face-to-face the principality of Haman.

I remember leaning over and whispering to my husband, "Nate, it's as though we are listening to Hitler himself talk callously about the Jews; it's that same spirit of Haman that demands their blood and annihilation…it dehumanizes humans." It was all I could do to weep and pray in tongues under my breath. As I sat praying in tongues silently, a security guard came over and abruptly and viciously grabbed hold of my shoulder.

Not a single person could hear me praying under my breath, not even Nate who was sitting right next to me. As I turned around, he was right up in my face glaring at me with an evil look in his eye. Then with a demonic voice, he growled, "You better be quiet, you are being disruptive!" Shocked, I looked at him, and before I could say anything, everyone around me jumped to my defense, "She hasn't made a single noise," they unanimously declared.

Ignoring them, and speaking again in a throaty, coarse voice with his face contorted, he said once more, "You need to shut up! You're disrupting everything!" At that I laughed, knowing exactly who I was talking to, not the man, but a spirit. I looked at him in the eye and said, "If you don't unhand me now, I'll make an even bigger scene." At that, he jumped in alarm, almost as though he were terrified at what I had just said, and backed away with a snarl on his face.

I find it profound, that while no one in the natural could hear me, the demonic realm could. My voice, though it was under my breath, was making a noise that was disrupting the powers of darkness and bringing confusion to the enemy's plans. We could even notice how things were being disrupted in the natural. The more I prayed while sitting up in the gallery, albeit under my breath, the more I noticed that the politicians became confused and stumbled over their own words. My prayers were interrupting the powers of darkness.

You need to remember that your prayers interrupt the powers of wickedness. It doesn't matter where you are, the enemy can hear what you are praying and it disrupts his plans, creating confusion within his own camp. When you pray, you are disrupting hell.

Sadly, however, that legislation did go through. The day it passed, legislators celebrated like it was a passage of their greatest victory. The premier of Queensland requested all of the buildings in our city, along with our bridges, be lit up in bright pink in celebration of passing this "woman's right" legislation. The Brisbane River that wraps its way around our CBD is speckled with bridges all the way along, and each were also lit up in pink. Not so ironically, the reflection upon our river that night was thus a pinkish/reddish hue, giving the appearance of a blood-spilled waterway.

God spoke to me the day it was passed, and said, "You've been aiming for the knees, you need to tackle the head. The head must be cut off before you'll see the rest of the giant fall." I knew immediately what He meant, I had to join my prayers and focus on seeing Roe v. Wade fall—the head of the giant. That's not to say I stopped fighting both in prayer and in action in Australia, but I knew then, that this demonic principality had to fall at the root.

Months later, I was invited to speak at a pro-life rally as we continued to stand against and pray for a reversal of this evil legislation. I was asked to speak for just 10 minutes and prepare a message. Knowing I would be standing next to the very Parliament where this spiritual battle played out, I prepared a message that would speak directly to these politicians, and call for their downfall, along with the demonic spirits that pervaded them. Then I planned to call on the name of Jesus and ask for His atoning Blood to wash over the sins of our state and nation.

That morning we showed up to the march and I was shocked (and slightly nervous) that the turnout was five times bigger than any pro-life rally before it—thousands in attendance compared to just hundreds the year before. The church had awakened and realized the battle they had permitted to rage in their silence. Thankfully now, they were awake, and they were loud. The march had wrapped its way through our city streets, closing off multiple streets, and finally we came to rest right next to the Queensland Parliament House.

With just five minutes to spare before I was due to be called up to speak, I was approached by some of the march organizers who were also fellow Christians. They told me they had looked through my speech and did not approve. Sternly, they told me I was not allowed to say the name of Jesus, lest I offended anyone in the crowd who was not a believer.

My heart sank, that was the whole reason I was there. Nate looked at me, "What are you going to do?" I sat in conflict within myself for a moment before someone grabbed my arm saying, "Follow me to the stage, it's your time to speak." I quickly leaned into Nate whispering into his ear, "Pray for me, I'm going rogue," before following them backstage. As I walked up on the stage, I was shaking. The march organizers stood right in front of me and I could feel the intimidation not to offend anyone.

Yet the moment I brought the microphone to my mouth, I felt a gust of courage rise up inside me. Under my breath, I whispered to the Holy Spirit, "Not by might, not by power, but by Your Spirit." I spoke every part of that speech I intended to release, and when the time came, I turned to the Parliament and released the mighty name of Jesus—commanding every demon in hell to fall under the power of His name. Needless to say, the march organizers were not impressed, and I'll likely never get an invitation to speak again under that leadership, but I did not come to please them. I came to call on the name of Jesus.

When I walked off the stage, an elderly man approached me. He was kind and gentle in nature, but had the appearance of a homeless man, and even smelled like one; yet he spoke with a clear authority. He looked at me and said, "The moment you declared the name of Jesus, I saw a principality fall from the top of the Parliament." Then he said something that shocked me, because very few knew our plans at the time to move to the United States or what God had said to me about the head of the giant. The man said, "You will go to the nation of America, and God will give you the head of the giant. Like Esther, you will go before the King and ask for the lives of the babies, and God is going to give them to you."

Shaken and now in tears, I looked at him in the eyes, and before I could say a sincere thank you, someone else tapped me on my shoulder. I turned around to see who had tapped me for a split second; and then turning back with the intention to say thank you to this man, he had completely vanished. With God as my witness, within a split second, the man was nowhere to be seen. To this day, I wholeheartedly believe he was an angel in disguise. Why was he dressed as a homeless person and even smelling like one, you may ask? Perhaps God was testing my heart to see if I would be willing to receive a word of the Lord from someone who didn't have the "perfect" appearance. All I can say is, I'll never forget that moment for as long as I live.

I share this story with you because in the world today where "cancel culture" is running prevalent, many daughters are walking around with spiritual masks covering their mouths. They have fallen prey to Haman's schemes, where his "multitude of noise" has silenced them into submission. Yet, it is the very sound of God's daughters who will cry out on the battlefield to King Jesus, "This is our request, this our desire, spare our children! Spare our nation." Our petition will usher in the resounding defeat of the enemy. Though you must be prepared to face resistance from both the world (the security guard in the gallery) and sadly even the church (the march organizers).

However, we are not on assignment of approval from them—we are on assignment by the Blood of the Lamb, and we are declaring His victory, drawing a line in the sand by His Blood that speaks a better word. It's going to look to others as though we are going rogue, but we are merely rejecting their opinions as the voice to follow. We are declaring *His testimony*. Yes, the Blood of Jesus works on our behalf, but we must *speak* it, make a *demand* upon it, and *seek* the answers *He has set* before us through it.

One final part to that story, the parliament member who introduced the "termination of pregnancy" legislation in Queensland would later be removed from her position because of "corruption in conduct." Just as I had prayed and declared, her schemes were exposed and her position fell, along with others. Though the overturning of this legislation is still in process, I am confident that the Blood of Jesus will speak a better word over Australia, and we will have the victory!

THE TABLE OF THE LAMB

Blood is a spiritual weapon, and the enemy knows it—that's why he goes after the blood of the innocent, the unborn. Yet, the Blood of Jesus is more powerful than any sin we could ever commit, and when we use it as our testimony, making petition by the Blood of Jesus, making a demand upon His redemption, it literally *unseats* the enemy from his high place of power and causes him to tremble.

Just watch what happened with Haman the moment Esther declared her testimony and exposed his schemes in Esther 7:6 (CSB): *"Esther answered, 'The adversary and enemy is this evil Haman.' Haman stood terrified before the king and queen."*

Do you see God's checkmate playing out here? The word of Esther's testimony caused the atonement to speak. Let's see what happens next in verses 7 and 8 (CSB):

> *The king arose in anger and went from where they were drinking wine to the palace garden. Haman remained to beg Queen Esther for his life because he realized the king was planning something terrible for him. Just then king returned from the palace garden to the banquet hall, Haman was falling on the couch where Esther was reclining. The king exclaimed, "Would he actually violate the queen while I am in the house?" As soon as the statement left the king's mouth, they covered Haman's face.*

What's profound is, many commentators and scholars alike believe that because of the timing overlapping with Passover, Esther actually prepared the Passover lamb for Haman.

There is so much more that I could unpack in these two verses alone, but for the sake of space, I want to direct your attention to *"they covered Haman's face."* When animals are about to be slaughtered, their faces are often covered. Haman was about to be led away to slaughter, and like the scapegoat that he was, his face was covered in finality of his evil schemes.

Finally, I want you to see who seals his fate:

> *Then Harbona, one of the eunuchs attending the king, said, "A sharpened pole reaching to a height of fifty cubits stands by Haman's house. He had it set up for Mordecai, who spoke up to help the king." The king said, "Impale him on it!"* (**Esther 7:9 NIV**)

It's often translated that this was a gallows, but the correct translation is an impaling pole, which in the modern metric system, reached up to 75 feet tall. The gruesome nature of this pole, would have meant Haman intended to throw Mordecai and the Jewish people onto it, resulting in a horrific and grisly slow death. They would have been thrown upon this sharp pole, alive, as their bodies slid down to the bottom where they would finally succumb to death.

Nauseating, I know. Yet this was the fate that Haman had "cast" upon himself; he ended up getting thrown over the cliff, so to speak, and his plans along with his life were broken into pieces. Now, this is not to suggest that we are contending for a similar fate for the enemies of God in our day, no. We are praying for their salvation, as we recognize that our battle is no longer against flesh and blood, but against principalities.

Harbona, one of the king's eunuchs (set-apart ones), became the voice that sealed the fate of the accuser. Harbona is a Persian name meaning "donkey-driver." Without going into too much detail, the donkey is symbolic in Scripture for being a carrier of God's Word. Think of when Jesus, *the Word*, was carried into Jerusalem on the back of a donkey before the completion work of His atonement upon the Cross. Therefore, it is no coincidence then that it is the donkey-driver who carries the testimony, the Word. Harbona reminded the king in this moment of Mordecai's report, and then Harbona ushers in the final blow that defeats the enemy. The king releases the word, and then Haman, along with all his sons and family, are thrown down and impaled upon the very trap he had set for Mordecai.

CHECKMATE.

ESTHER'S DECREE

BIBLE READING: ESTHER 8

On January 22, 1973, a decree went forth from the Supreme Court that would echo its statutes across all 50 of the United States. Like a sound wave, this one decree reverberated around the world, drumming the sound of its deadly declaration into legislations of other countries, including my own homeland of Australia. It was the ruling of Roe v. Wade—the legal passage of abortion and innocent bloodshed—modern-day child sacrifice.

In its wake would lie the blood of more than 63 million children in the United States alone.[1] Other countries would soon follow the declaration of this decree, implementing their own deathly decrees, in supposed proclamations of women's rights. Celebrated like a victory in each new legislation, many women cheered at their newfound "reproductive freedom." The decree was born of a lie. The defendant, "Jane Doe," would later admit that she was manipulated by the female lawyers who preyed upon her struggle and story to usher in this ruling. Jane Doe—real name, Norma McCorvey—would go on to have the baby that the shrewd lawyers argued for the right to terminate. Before Norma's death in 2017, she gave her life to the Lord and became adamantly pro-life.

This decree was not conceived alone. The ruling was spawned through the declarations of other insidious decrees. This far-reaching ruling didn't start out like the monster we know it to be today. It was developed through seed form; at first, tiny ideas that didn't seem quite so deceitful, small concepts that over time were left unopposed, grew and morphed into a leviathan of sorts—a dragon with multiple heads. Ideas like "women's liberation," which started out, mostly innocent with legitimate reasonings for women to vote and buy property, quickly grew into lust for power, hatred of all men and greed for self.

I would submit that the women who fought for the rights to vote in the late 1800s would be horrified at what women are fighting for today. Noble, righteous women like Sojourner Truth, who, upon being freed from slavery, immediately sought the freedom of her own son. Sojourner would weep at the women of today who hold their signs not to free their children, but to free themselves of their children by the passage of death.

I would argue that the majority of women who are praised as "the first wave of feminists" were not at all feminists as we know them today. They were abolitionists who valued the role of mothers and the bedrock foundation of family; they did not hate their men but merely sought basic human rights.

Feminism of today was birthed largely out of the second wave from the late 1960s; and upon careful study, we find that there were decrees written by a group of feminists, that much like the decree of Roe v Wade, are still echoing into our modern day. These decrees helped to birth, ironically, the declaration of Roe v. Wade, the sexual revolution (with some help from the dark teachings of Alfred Kinsey and others like him, but that is a whole other story), and the breakdown of the family unit.

Found within the "Redstockings Manifesto"—a group of bitter, angry women who despised men and sought to destroy the downfall of family—we find their decrees, summarized in short as follows:

I. Women are uniting to achieve final liberation from male supremacy.

II. Women are oppressed as breeders, sex objects, domestic servants and cheap labor.

III. We have lived intimately with our oppressors, in isolation from each other... this creates the illusion that a woman's relationship with her man is a matter of interplay...when in reality, every such relationship is a class relationship.

IV. We identify the agents of our oppression as men. All men. Male supremacy is the oldest, most basic form of domination. We do not need to change ourselves, but to change men.

V. We are committed to achieving internal democracy. We will do whatever is necessary to ensure that every woman in our movement has an equal chance to participate, assume responsibility, and develop her political potential.

VI. We call on all our sisters to unite with us in struggle.

VII. We call on all men to give up their male privilege and support women's liberation in the interest of our humanity and their own.

In fighting for our liberation we will always take the side of women against their oppressors. We will not ask what is "revolutionary" or "reformist," only what is good for women.

The time for individual skirmishes has passed. This time we are going all the way.

July 7, 1969

To truly understand what was being declared here, we need to look closely at the words being used. Rather than saying "mother," the Redstockings declared women to be "breeders." They viewed the gift of motherhood as nothing more than an animalistic sentence of captivity. Homemakers were deemed as "domestic servants" and "cheap labor." They declared the sacred relationship of a husband and wife as a class relationship—a caste system where a woman lived in servitude to her husband, both for sex and every other conceivable notion. Every man on planet Earth was declared an oppressor, unless of course, he wanted to deny his masculinity, which they required he be treated like a woman by his fellow male companions.

They declared, "we will only ask what is good for women." Notice how satanic this statement is—it immediately eliminates God's design for us as females to be nurturers of others (not withholding care for ourselves, of course); but therein lies the root for the head of abortion that would grow from this beast. "My body, my choice," because only "I" matter.

In one foul declaration, the feminists of the Redstockings sent out a proclamation that, like the waves of the sea, would crash upon society again and again, until the very fabrics of morality, truth, and family would be corroded away. According to a study by the Pew Research Center, the United States has the highest rate of single parent families in the world.[2] "The U.S. Census Bureau today released estimates showing there were 10.9 million one-parent family groups with a child under the age of 18 in 2022. Data from the annual release of America's Families and Living Arrangements also show that 80% of one-parent family groups were maintained by a mother."[3]

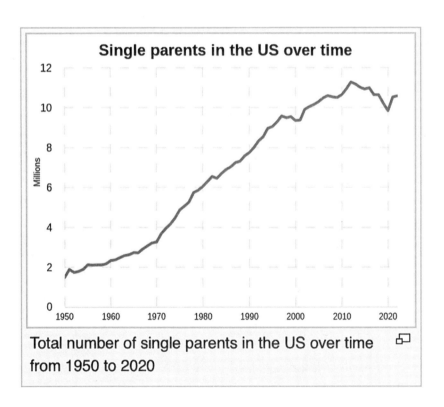

Total number of single parents in the US over time from 1950 to 2020

This graph from the Pew Research Center is chilling.[4] Though there was already a slow rise beginning in 1950, look how rapidly the numbers increased through and after the 1960s. What's more, the number of single-parent families rapidly increased during the 1960s. Could it be that this is in part the result of the Redstockings Manifesto? I believe so.

I must stress before I move on with this point—this is in no way to condemn single mothers or even single fathers. I cannot even fathom the stress of raising children alone. I just want to say you are doing such an incredible job, Mama. The Father sees you, and He is your strength. You have rewards in Heaven that none of us have. This is no way a reflection of condemnation upon single mothers and I emphasize this boldly—you are *not* a failure. We are praying for you and believe that the Lord is the Father to your children in the absence of theirs.

For those reading this who are not a single mother, I encourage you to find a single mama in your life and take this moment to reach out to her and see if she needs help. Find out how she is and what can be done for her. Maybe pay for a spa treatment while the kids are at school. Maybe deliver a bag full of groceries. I believe the Lord wants us to surround these mamas, as we overturn this decree by helping pour healing over families once again.

My point is though, could it be that the United States and other nations that have followed suit in these feminist Ishtar decrees, are still living under the curse of their declarations? Could it be that this curse has not been dealt with and broken? You might ask, "Aren't we free from the curse?"

The Blood of Jesus certainly sets us free from the curse, but it must be applied; and as I am about to show you through Esther, a new decree must be declared. I don't believe that has been properly done—at least not as a whole body of Christ. Could it be that we will see the reversal of the breakdown of family and healing will pour out as we begin to release a new proclamation over families, husbands and wives, and the children of tomorrow's generations?

I also want to add that many women have indeed been abused by men, and I don't want you to assume that I am for abuse of any kind. My opposition to the Redstockings Manifesto is not to suggest that I am for men who abuse women—by all means, hear my resounding NO!

I recognize that a measure, albeit a small measure, of what they were saying, was founded in a portion of truth; some men (notice I'm saying some, not all) do indeed abuse women. God condemns such actions; women were not created by Him to be slaves of men, sexual or otherwise. God created us equal, unique in our distinctions and gifts, but equal to stand beside one another and support each other—He created Eve from the side of Adam, not his feet.

If you have never had a man who supports you, daughter, I pray that the Holy Spirit would first heal you of any grief, pain, and betrayal that men have caused in your life. Second, I pray the Holy Spirit would bring a man of righteousness into your life, one who resembles the character of Mordecai, who paces the courtyard of your heart for your protection.

LIES ON TOP OF LIES

Back to the Redstockings Manifesto, it's important to discern the lies within this declaration. I highlight this because many good Christian women of today are wholly unaware of this declaration and are actually partnering and supporting modern feminism. Or perhaps they are aware, but through open wounds from men they have received this manifesto, in whole, as truth. It's important we address this, because we have to dismantle the enemy's lies over God's daughters.

Let's look back for a moment at the initial fall of humanity that came through Eve. Notice that Eve leaned into the whispers of a lying serpent. Her ears recognized a half-truth, for the serpent cunningly asked her, *"Did God really say, 'You must not eat from any tree of the garden?'"* (Genesis 3:1 NIV).

Satan's schemes (remember the word *schemes* from earlier chapters) are the same then as they are today. Determined, pre-set, predictable. If he played this game on Eve in the Garden of Eden, we better wise up to the fact that he is still attempting to perform this stunt on us women today. With all the gifts of food given to Eve in the Garden, the serpent made her question that perhaps she needed more. She may have wondered, *Just maybe God didn't really say I couldn't eat from this tree?*

Today, we see this doubt playing out through the monstrous head of feminism. Many women are saying, "I need more. I need more than the gifts given to me. I want to eat from the tree that is not mine to eat from"—rather than delighting in the roles God has given us as nurturers, warriors in our own right, helpers and bearers of life, both in the natural and in the spirit.

Another important side note: I say all this not to condemn or grieve women who have struggled with infertility, as I recognize this is a robbery of the enemy. We are standing with you for the fulfillment of your promises as well. The serpent today has convinced the daughters of this generation that they must take on the roles of men. They declare, "We are nothing if we can't have everything. Let's eat from every tree we desire, even that of the roles of men."

Once more, allow me to reiterate that I see nothing wrong with women working in the workforce. Where I see the lie is when this desire becomes the only goal in life. Women in the world today are choosing a "career" over the "gift" of motherhood. Can we have both? Absolutely. Yet when the overarching theme in society is to do away completely with motherhood, we must ask what has gone wrong?

I encourage you to search on social media to see what I am referring to. There are multitudes of social media sites under the topic "childless or child-free by choice." This is not just a decision to not have children. If you dig a little deeper into the comments, you will see there is a deep resentment toward children. This is Ishtar at work once again.

Furthermore, most of the women who despise children have multiple photos of their pets displayed on their individual pages. Dogs and cats fill the space of their nurturing instincts that should be for children. Once more, I'll make another side note here, as I know I'm hitting a lot of "sore points" in today's societal norms. Yet as I promised you, I'm not here to tickle ears.

I will say, however, I love animals. We have our own pets that we nurture and tend to as fur babies—but they are not humans. They don't take the place of my children; however, many in society have chosen otherwise. We must recognize that a decree has been declared and many women have listened, most have unknowingly submitted and have indeed fallen prey to its curse.

Could it be as well that men too have unknowingly submitted to these lies? Men who used to stand and protect their families are leaving the responsibility of fatherhood by the droves. Could this curse that was supposed to "liberate" women have done the polar opposite? Attempting to be their own gods, many women threw away the decrees and right order of God in the hopes to right a wrong—but doing so without the Lord has resulted in the downfall of society. We have traded the truth of our identity as women—our God-given gifts as life-bearers—for a lie. The lie that we can be exactly like men, and the gift of being a mother is nothing more than a breeding program in a zoo.

CONFUSION AND CHAOS

The Redstockings got what they asked for. They wanted to be completely equal to men without recognizing that in value, we are equal—but our identities are different. However, they wanted it all. Now? Men are competing in women's sports, beating them ruthlessly on the grounds of the playing field—both naturally and spiritually. By deducing the God-given role of men, they have demanded and succeeded in feminizing their masculinity.

Confused men are now trading their identities and parading around in women's clothes. Reducing our womanhood down to a costume. The enemy is spitting in our faces when they declare that there is no such thing as breast-feeding and renaming pregnant mothers as birthing people, attempting to redefine the definition of woman and mother.

Do you see the lies manifesting in every realm of our society today? Many of the lies and illusions we see demonstrated today, I believe, stem back to this manifesto—a declaration schemed up by the principality of Ishtar. This manifesto also gave way for the sexual revolution of the 1970s where women picked up the books written by the radical women of the Redstockings movement and believed an ideology that touted, "Sleep with whoever you want, whenever you want." An ideology that supposedly freed women in the bedroom, but in reality only more deeply bound them to sexual promiscuity.

Then, of course, with this blatant sexual revolution came the decree of Roe v. Wade in 1973. A cunning tactic of the enemy to use women's liberation to wipe out an entire generation of children, destroy their mothers in the process, and dismantle the foundations of family that are the bedrock of any healthy and thriving society—all from one decree. Today, those decrees continue to be taught in the children's classrooms where sexual liberation leads to perverted ends.

A movement for "liberation" from the "age of consent" is currently underway. You read that right. All these ungodly declarations have grown more vile and contemptuous over the years to now when pedophilia is on the rise. The sexual revolution and "women's liberation" has morphed into further abuse of women through pornography, which is a growing demon of its own. Need I go on?

Women have handed over the role of gatekeepers of their home; men too have surrendered their roles as guardians of their families.

Men—as Mordecai did—should be standing guard at the gates of their families. But instead, many have been "released" through feminism, to sleep around promiscuously. Both men and women need to take up their guards.

A study through recent history reveals these death decrees have indeed broken down the family unit. And dare I say it all came through the open gates, the trojan horse of the second and third waves of feminism. I believe that it is the voice of God's righteous daughters in this hour that are anointed to overturn these lies.

"When will it all stop?" I will tell you when. When the Esthers arise with the decrees of God and declare a new declaration of life over our children and the coming generations. There was just one Esther in the Old Testament; but in this hour, God is raising up an army of Esthers, daughters mantled with her robe, for the hour at hand requires us all. Each daughter will decree a *new thing* to overturn the magnitude of decrees that have gone forth.

I am reminded of this verse from the New King James Version of Job 22:28 that says, *"You will also declare a thing, and it will be established for you; so light will shine on your ways."*

The Hebrew word used for *declare* here is *gazar*[5] and it means to cut down, cut off, decree, divide, slice off. We need a revelation that our decrees *slice off* and *cut down* the enemy's decrees over our generations today. Hebrews 4:12 from the New Living Translation similarly tells us, *"For the word of God is alive and powerful. It is sharper than the sharpest two-edged sword, cutting between soul and spirit, between joint and marrow. It exposes our innermost thoughts and desires."*

Do you see what I'm seeing? When we make a *new* declaration over the generations of today through the Word of God, we are cutting through and slicing off the enemy's plans. So my question to you today is, "What are you decreeing? Are you making declarations that are in agreement with the enemy's plans when you make statements such as, 'There's no hope for this generation!'"

Or are you making declarations of the new thing that God is longing to pour out over them? Declarations like, "It may look hopeless, but God has marked this generation for the greatest outpouring of all time!" It is past time that we put an end to the decrees of Haman where the likes of the Redstockings, the sexual revolution, and Roe v. Wade have long declared death over our children, our families, and the coming generations.

Today, we are called to annihilate these demonic decrees once and for all. It is time that we intervene for our children and take back the territory of the family and the nations, and bring them into the subjugation of the finished work of the Cross where the Blood of Jesus cries out on their behalf and declares, "IT IS FIN-ISHED!" over Haman's decrees.

HAMAN'S DECREE CUT DOWN

I want you to see something profound in this portion of Scripture in Esther 8 as she moves to intervene on behalf of the Jews. Haman had just been hung, his body likely still hanging on the tree; he and his family annihilated. However, his decree of assassination over the Jews was still resounding, echoing with authority in the atmosphere. Though Haman was gone, his decree was still withstanding.

Have you ever wondered why the king didn't just revoke Haman's decree? Esther 3:12-13 (CSB) explains why:

> *The royal scribes were summoned on the thirteenth day of the first month, and the order was written exactly as Haman commanded. It was intended for the royal satraps, the governors of each of the provinces, and the officials of each ethnic group and written for each province in its own script and to each ethnic group in its own language. It was written in the name of King Ahasuerus and sealed with the royal **signet ring**. Letters were sent by couriers to each of the royal provinces telling the officials to destroy, kill, and annihilate all the Jewish people—young and old, women and children—and plunder their possessions on a single day, the thirteenth day of Adar, the twelfth month.*

First to highlight in this text is the signet ring. In ancient times it was a symbol of authority and ownership. Haman ensured that his decrees were sealed with the wax seal of the king's signet ring. This established that the order could not be revoked, even by the king himself; therefore, a new decree had to be written to overrule this one.

Before we get into overturning the decree though, I want you to see something else. Who did Haman specifically write his order to? The royal satraps and governors of each of the provinces. *Satrap* in Hebrew means "protector of the realm"[6] and *governor* in Hebrew means "lord of the district."[7] Haman was summoning the demonic principalities of regions, and in a similar way in our day, the decrees of death that have been released have summoned the demonic protectors and lords of spiritual realms. Think about it—the decree of the Redstockings has largely affected the United States. Why not the same for other countries? Because the decree was sent out over this region and the enemy—principalities and lords of the spiritual realms—has remained in authority because it has not been revoked. Furthermore, Haman's declaration to annihilate the Jews was written into order on the thirteenth day of Nisan, the first month. This declaration was to be initiated on the thirteenth day of Adar, the twelfth month.

One thing specifically makes an impression here, the number 13. Additionally, the months of Adar and Nisan, which you will remember from the chapters of Haman. For now, I want to briefly focus on the thirteenth—a day that Haman both wrote his decree and planned for his decree. Everything has significance in Scripture, even numbers. Many Christians will naively assume that studying the Hebrew meaning of a number means you are looking into numerology. This could not be further from the truth.

Remember, satan mimics and mocks the designs of God, and numerology is nothing more than a devious mockery and imitation of God's language within numbers. In ancient times, the Hebrew language did not use numbers, they counted with their alphabet. So the thirteenth number was represented by the thirteenth letter of the Hebraic alphabet. I hope I'm not losing you here, but bear with me because there is an incredible hidden message within this thirteenth day.

The thirteenth Hebrew letter is the letter *mem*. Each Hebrew letter has a pictographic, and the picture for *mem* represents chaos, immersion, or water, the womb and blood. This letter also connects to Moses and the Messiah as it is the first letter for each, pointing to deliverance. (Not to forget of course, Mordecai.)

These details reveal to us several things: 13 points to the Old and New Covenants in Scripture. The Old representing the old order and the need for the sacrifice of animals to temporarily subside the chaos of sin. Then, under Jesus His Blood immersed us into the New where Jesus would become the firstborn among the New order. Why does all this matter? Because we see here yet another portrayal of Jesus within Esther—where He becomes the signet ring of our authority today to revoke the plans of Haman.

Haman's plans were foiled from the moment he set his heart against God's people. Once more, he unknowingly positioned himself for that checkmate and fell headfirst into the very trap he had laid out for the Jews. He was prophetically portraying the coming Messiah through the declaration of Esther and Mordecai.

Now I want to turn to Esther 8:1-2 (CSB):

> *That same day King Ahasuerus awarded Queen Esther the estate of Haman, the enemy of the Jews. Mordecai entered the king's presence because Esther had revealed her relationship to Mordecai. The king removed his signet ring he had recovered from Haman and gave it to Mordecai, and Esther put him in charge of Haman's estate.*

I simply love these verses. It is such a beautiful portrait of redemption. The first thing the king does following Haman's execution is to award Esther Haman's estate. The Hebrew word for *awarded* in this verse is *nathan*[8] and it means to "deliver up, bestow and appoint." Esther was delivered up what was rightfully hers. She then appoints and bestows it to Mordecai, the rightful owner.

This is a powerful picture of the coming redemption through Jesus, where God would once more use a woman, through Mary, to redeem the territory the enemy has stolen. Today, the Lord is doing this once again; and as I have said multiple times—not just through one woman, through every daughter in this hour.

One other tidbit of intriguing detail here is the word for Haman's estate, the Hebrew word *bayith*,[9] and while it can mean the obvious "house and land," it can also mean "treasury" and "daughter." Do you see what I see? The decrees of Haman have bound a treasury of God's daughters all around the earth—and in this hour God is using His daughters, you and me, to set them all free. And once free, we hand them back into the rightful hands of Jesus, our Mordecai.

THE GREAT REVERSAL

The king also recovered his king's signet ring, and he personally handed this to Mordecai. Interestingly, the signet ring is also tied to Jesus. Allow me to show you this one significant verse in Haggai 2:23 (NIV) that says:

> "On that day," declares the Lord Almighty, "I will take you, my servant Zerubbabel son of Shealtiel," declares the Lord, "and I will make you like my signet ring, for I have chosen you," declares the Lord Almighty.

I'm sure you're wondering, *But how does this tie in to Jesus and even Mordecai?* Without going too deep into a diversion here, Zerubbabel was yet another foreshadow of Christ, and this verse is a prophetic declaration that Jesus would become the signet ring of authority over the nations. Let's come back to this in a moment, because there is something else profound that I must show you.

Let's first read what happens next with Esther and Mordecai in Esther 8:3-8 (BSB):

> *And once again, Esther addressed the king. She fell at his feet weeping and begged him to revoke the evil scheme of Haman the Agagite, which he had devised against the Jews.*
>
> *The king extended the gold scepter toward Esther, and she arose and stood before the king. "If it pleases the king," she said, "and if I have found favor in his sight, and the matter seems proper to the king, and I am pleasing in his sight, may an order be written to revoke the letters that the scheming Haman son of Hammedatha, the Agagite, wrote to destroy the Jews in all the king's provinces. For how could I bear to see the disaster that would befall my people? How could I bear to see the destruction of my kindred?"*
>
> *So King Xerxes said to Esther the Queen and Mordecai the Jew, "Behold, I have given Haman's estate to Esther, and he was hanged on the gallows because he attacked the Jews. Now you may write in the king's name as you please regarding the Jews, and seal it with the royal signet ring. For a decree that is written in the name of*

the king and sealed with the royal signet ring cannot be revoked."

I want you to take note here that to overturn Haman's decree, a new decree had to be written, by none other than Mordecai. This new decree required the signet ring of the king's authority that was now given to Mordecai. Then in Esther 8:9 (BSB) we read:

At once the royal scribes were summoned, and on the twenty-third day of the third month (the month of Sivan), they recorded all of Mordecai's orders to the Jews and to the satraps, governors, and princes of the 127 provinces from India to Cush—writing to each province in its own script, to every people in their own language, and to the Jews in their own script and language.

You will notice that Mordecai overturned the decree by addressing the same principalities that Haman had called upon. Only this time, Mordecai was telling them you've lost this battle. What's more, the 127 provinces represent the nations of the earth (derived from the meaning of the Hebraic numbers). Mordecai sent out a new decree that overthrew the previous one.

Then if we look at the month he summoned the scribes, it was the third month, the month of Sivan. *Sivan* in Hebrew means "season and time." This was God colliding a *kairos* with a *chronos*—a divinely ordered season of time, which I believe we are also in right at this moment.

God is summoning His daughters for such a time as this, and we, too, are being called to write and declare a new declaration over the earth—to send out the *new* order of Jesus to every province, in our own languages, and make this declaration to the principalities that have been governing over our regions: "A reversal is in play. God is in motion. He is overturning the decrees that have destroyed the woman, the man, the child, and the family, and He is ushering in the greatest harvest known to mankind."

One final thing I want you to see in this context is the twenty-third day that Mordecai's new declaration was written. For larger numbers in Hebrew, their meanings are often combined through their total sum. For example 23 is the sum of the number 10 and 13. The number 10 can mean "perfect order," and the number 13, as we discovered earlier, can point us to the New Covenant, the finished work of the Cross. Another way to study what a number means in Scripture is to search its correlating chapters or verses, and additionally the number of times something is mentioned in Scripture.

Upon this research, I found that Adam and Eve had 23 daughters. What could this be pointing to? I believe this points prophetically to a new generation of daughters that God is raising up to right the wrongs of Eve—in our present context—radical feminism. In addition, I discovered that Jezebel was mentioned 23 times in Scripture, once more revealing that this twenty-third day of Sivan was prophetically declaring that the counterfeit voice of women in this hour shall be overturned by the voices of God's true daughters, His Esthers arising. Finally, we will do so by the signet ring of the authority of Jesus, our Mordecai.

Remember the verse that spoke of Zerubbabel and his signet ring of authority? Look at the verse number—Haggai 2:23. Jesus now holds this signet ring of authority and we, like Esther, have been given permission to write a new decree through Him. God has written a tapestry of incredible detail for us within the book of Esther, so that we can not only find hope in our present day, but also keys to wield the authority of the finished work of the Cross, the Blood.

Mordecai reversed the decree by writing this new declaration:

> *The king's edict gave the Jews in each and every city the right to assemble and defend themselves, to destroy, kill and annihilate every ethnic and provincial army hostile to them, including women and children, and to take their possessions as spoils of war. This would take place on a single day throughout all the provinces of King Ahasuerus, on the thirteenth day of the twelfth month, the month Adar. A copy of the text, issued as law throughout every province, was distributed to all the peoples so that the Jews could be ready to avenge themselves against their enemies on that day. The couriers rode out in haste on their royal horses at the king's urgent command. The law was also issued in the fortress of Susa* (**Esther 8:11-14 CSB**).

Before we move on to the final chapters of Esther and the final chapter of this book, I want to highlight just a few more details here. Mordecai reversed the death decree on the same day that was assigned for their annihilation—the thirteenth day of Adar. You may recall that *Adar* means "strength and power." They were moved from a place of weakness and vulnerability to one of strength and power.

Could it be that through our declarations today, we will see the overturning of broken and weak families into strong and resilient ones? Could it be that we will witness God's daughters take back their rightful positions, and God's sons as the head of their homes too? Could we see the greatest outpouring of healing from the Holy Spirit, along with a harvest of prodigals into the Kingdom, all through the writing of a new declaration by the signet ring of the Blood of Jesus? I firmly believe so.

Yet as it is written in these verses, the declaration went forth at the king's urgent command. We are in an hour of urgency, and we must recognize that if we don't hasten and revoke the edicts of the death decrees past, our children may not have strength to fight back in the days to come. However, my hope is entirely in Jesus; and I firmly believe He is awakening both sons and daughters in this hour of urgency to raise the banner high and shout from the corners of the streets and into the gateways of every city that a new decree is being established this day. The decree of the finished work of Jesus.

Finally, I want you to see these last details. Esther 8:15-17 (BSB) says:

> *Mordecai went out from the presence of the king in royal garments of blue and white, with a large gold crown and a purple robe of fine linen. And the city of Susa shouted and rejoiced. For the Jews it was a time of light and gladness, of joy and honor. In every province and every city, wherever the king's edict and decree reached, there was joy and gladness among the Jews, with feasting and celebrating. And many of the people*

of the land themselves became Jews, because the fear of the Jews had fallen upon them.

Mordecai was dressed in royal garments of blue and white. Blue signifies the Word of God, it represents the glory of God and the law of the Lord. It's profound that Mordecai walked out from the presence of the king wrapped in the new order; or prophetically, it was a picture of the New Covenant to come through Jesus. Next, white speaks of righteousness and the finished work of the Cross. The gold crown portrays the authority of Christ, and the purple robe of fine linen depicts His royalty, honor and priesthood. Finally, purple additionally represents the Proverbs 31 woman. Proverbs 31:22 (ESVUK) says, *"her clothing is fine linen and purple."*

Daughter, God has mantled you in this critical hour with the royal robes of Esther. You have been given the signet ring of the authority of Jesus—your Mordecai—and it is time for you to declare a new edict over your life, your family, your children, and your children's children. It is time to make haste and overturn the rule of Haman.

NOTES

1. "National Right to Life Releases Ninth Annual Report: The State of Abortion in the United States," January 31, 2022, *National Right to Life;* https://www.nrlc.org/communications/releases/2022/013122sausreport/; accessed April 14, 2024.

2. Stephanie Kramer, "U.S. has world's highest rate of children living in single-parent households," *Pew Research Center,* December 12, 2019; https://www.pewresearch.org/short-reads/2019/12/12/u-s-children-more-likely-than-children-in-other-countries-to-live-with-just-one-parent/; accessed April 14, 2024.

3. "Estimates on America's Families and Living Arrangements," *United States Census Bureau,* Census Bureau Press Release Number CB22-TPS.99, November 17, 2022; https://www.census.gov/newsroom/press-releases/2022/americas-families-and-living-arrangements.html; accessed April 14, 2024.

4. Single parents in the United States; https://en.m.wikipedia.org/wiki/Single_parents_in_the_United_States; accessed May 22, 2024.

5. Strong's Hebrew Concordance #1504.

6. Strong's Hebrew Concordance #323.

7. Strong's Hebrew Concordance #6346.

8. Strong's Hebrew Concordance #5414.

9. Strong's Hebrew Concordance #1004.

END-TIME VICTORY

BIBLE READING: ESTHER 9-10

In 2023, a movie burst onto the scene that in effect, took the world by storm. Few films have gained the level of hype and frenzy that this one managed to garner—and no wonder, it was smothered in pink dust and cherry glitter. Visually appealing, colorful and vibrant, it was by all outward appearances, fun and whimsical. Afterall, it played into the heart of every little girl, young and old, who has ever loved her dolls and Barbies in her childhood.

The *Barbie* movie grossed number one in box offices worldwide, and "pink parties" were all the rage, with friends and families turning their cinema-going into a special event to watch the premiere. I too assumed it was a sweet and carefree movie and looked forward to taking my girls to see it on a night out together—until I saw some of the advertisements.

I will be the first to say, I loved playing with my Barbies as a little girl and my own daughters have owned this doll. I have fond memories of setting up her "dream house" and pretending to have her put her babies to sleep, then cooking dinner as Ken arrived home in his car, giving her a kiss on the cheek. Mine was the stereotypical Barbie as displayed in the film.

Before I step on some toes, or rather, heels, I realize many women went and saw this movie, with their daughters in tow, and own Barbies for their own daughters as I do too. But before you run to the assumption that this is a judgment against you, it is not. It is my heart to uncover the cunning and deceptive ways in which the enemy of our souls is captivating an entire generation.

If we are going to engage as Esther, we must be willing to lay everything down as Esther did. And before you throw this book down in its final chapter declaring, "She's overexaggerating," please listen and ask the Holy Spirit to reveal to you what I'm saying.

I shared a post on social media after researching the underlying messages within this Barbie film and I was utterly amazed at the response. My audience is largely, if not entirely, a Christian following of women—however, the comments on this post, did not reflect that at all. My post simply said, "In a world of Barbies, be an Esther." And, "In a world of Barbies, be a Deborah." I witnessed firsthand, just how emotionally attached many women had grown to this film.

I must ask, how could the declaration of being a godly woman over a worldly one, somehow be offensive? Yet, it was. We ought to be acutely attentive in this hour to keep our allegiances to the Cross alone—even if that means laying down a movie we love, a song we enjoy listening to, or an artist we adore. We can have no room for compromise as we carry the mantle of Esther.

I was labeled a Pharisee and a judgmental clown for posting those two comments; and while labels don't affect me whatsoever—I only have one I adhere to: a daughter of the King—it opened my eyes to the dark, underlying spiritual principalities at work within this film. If there is any resemblance of evil, even in the most subtle of forms, even if it's covered in pink glitter, we must turn our backs on it. For all that glitters, is *not* gold. Ephesians 5:11 (NIV) instructs us: *"Have nothing to do with the fruitless deeds of darkness, but rather expose them."*

While it may seem out of place to speak of a movie about Barbie in a book that is central to Esther, I want to take you on a little journey to show you that this is a prime example of how the enemy is operating in our day—and it is also an example of how the Lord is going to use the enemy's plans for God's glory.

You may be wondering, *How could this pretty, fun, colorful, and "harmless" film have anything dark within it?* Well…where to begin? Yes, I have watched it, merely to gain a deeper understanding of what is being said and portrayed. (I watched with gritted teeth I might add.) So I'm not speaking from an ignorant standpoint. And as you will find, what I am about to share with you is intrinsic to the end-time church and the victorious bride—and it all ties into Esther.

The film's introduction tells us everything we need to know from the get-go. The filmmakers were strategic in visually creating an opening scene that immediately depicted their underlying messages. In the opening scene we see a group of little girls, no older than five, vintage dressed in the kind of clothes my own mother used to dress me in for Sunday School. Pinafores and floral dresses with puffy sleeves and Peter Pan collars, frilly socks, with bows in their hair. Sweet and innocent. The backdrop of this scene is in contrast, not so sweet—a red dusty desert with scorching sun beating down on the surroundings. This group of little girls are playing, albeit morbidly, in the dust with baby dolls.

The narrator's voice enters, saying, *"Since the beginning of time, since the first little girl ever existed, there have been dolls."* Her voice, soothing and inviting, like a trustworthy grandmother. She goes on to narrate, *"But the dolls were always and forever, baby dolls. The girls who played with them could only ever play at being mothers. Which can be fun, at least, for a while, anyway."*

Her voice changes, now sinister and demeaning, as she says, *"Ask your mother."* Then Barbie appears, almost like a giant, golden statue. She towers above the little girls, clothed in her first design of attire from the 1960s. She stands tall among them, mysterious, mesmerizing, inviting. They look up at her, gazing at her beauty, and with jaws dropped aghast, victorious music fills the screen as the little girls pick up their baby dolls and begin smashing them onto other baby dolls. Images fill the screen of baby dolls' heads exploding, baby dolls flying, and then smashing into a million pieces as Barbie watches on.

Surely this was just satire, some might declare in defense. Let's find out.

A closer look at the opening scene reveals that this was a parody from Stanley Kubrick's film, *2001: A Space Odyssey—the Dawn of Man.* Kubrick's film depicts the enlightenment, or awakening of apes as they supposedly evolve from their primitive state into understanding how to fight for themselves. *A Space Odyssey* opens with an identical backdrop to Barbie's. Only in a twisted parallel, instead of little girls playing with their baby dolls, there are primitive apes picking their toes and eating dirt from the ground. Where the apes are drinking by hand out of the water, Barbie's parody displays the little girls offering cups of water to their babies. Do you see the messaging here? It is meant to depict that the desire for motherhood is primitive.

What's most disturbing is the apes have an awakening through an alien monolith that appears in the form of a pyramid, and they too begin smashing things—bones of dead animals to be precise— and they discover how to use the bones as weapons. How alarming.

The parallel created in Barbie was meant to display an "awakening" of young girls everywhere. Not an awakening to truth, but an enlightenment to Barbie, or to a monolith. Remember Ishtar? She sacrifices her own children to save herself. And today her children have become her weapons of war, sacrificed to this demon entity, as opposed to the mother standing as a weapon of war against the monolith.

Was the Barbie movie truly just displaying a fun and harmless parody? Or was this a strategic message at the hands of a principality in hiding? Given the extreme feminist undertones throughout the entire movie, I would argue it is the latter. Another opening scene reveals Barbie driving down the street in her perfect Barbie world that is ruled over only by Barbie women. In her pink car, she passes another Barbie, named Midge. Midge is pregnant, and the narrator immediately declares, "Let's not focus too much on Midge, Mattel discontinued her because a pregnant doll is just weird." Was this movie distinctly mocking motherhood, family, and the role of good men? Considering children learn through play, and they form central understandings of life through their play, I would say so.

Some would argue that there are other themes within the movie that suggest otherwise saying, "There is the storyline of a mother trying to gain back her relationship with her daughter, so this is certainly not the conclusion." And, "They balance things out to a degree in the end." I would propose to remember this: the enemy always mixes a lie with a sliver of truth. If he were to come out attacking mothers, degrading motherhood, and the desire to have babies without portraying a caring mother in the mix, as well as degrading men without letting them have a tiny comeback in the end, there would be a complete uproar.

But no, the enemy is far smarter than that, much more cunning than we give him credit. He knows that for a lie to embed and sustain itself, he must also sprinkle it with a micro measure of truth—a bite-size ingredient of intrinsic truth, as watered down as it may be, that causes the mind not to question the sinister nature of the messaging.

IDOLS HIDING IN HIGH PLACES

Consider the fairy tale of Little Red Riding Hood. The little girl is sent on a mission to deliver cake to her sickly grandmother. Upon her journey through the woods, she encounters a wolf. At their meeting, the wolf quickly extracts information from her about the grandmother's whereabouts, and discreetly he journeys there ahead of the little girl.

Upon the wolf's arrival at the grandmother's house, he devours the grandmother and then clothes himself in the grandmother's attire. Little Red Riding Hood immediately notices something is askew with her grandmother, though she is not completely alert to the imminent danger because his clothes are trustworthy. "What a deep voice you have," she declares. "The better to greet you with," responds the wolf. "Goodness, what big eyes you have," says the girl. "All the better to see you with," responds the wolf. "But...what big hands you have!" The little girl is becoming more aware of the danger, but not soon enough. "The better to embrace you with," he replies. "What a big mouth you have," she stutters in alarm. "The better to eat you with!" And the wolf jumps out of the bed and eats her as well.

Though just a fairy tale, this fable illustrates to us the exact way the enemy operates. He clothes himself in what appears to be truth. He makes himself appear less sinister and malevolent. Like the wolf in the grandmother's clothing, he at first appears friendly, common, and trustworthy. Through catchy songs, mesmerizing artists, sparkly movies, and appealing games on phones and play stations, he infiltrates our minds and the minds of our children— not always blaringly obvious at first, but with a trickle of lies, he manipulates. Little by little until entire school systems and universities, governments and media alike, are completely held within the grasp of his deceptions.

He convinces the world he doesn't exist, but he and his cohorts of demon principalities hide in our day and age atop the high places of entertainment, government, and education. Where they were worshipped atop temples with idols and statues in the days of the Bible, today they have adapted to the modern world, realizing that the modern world would not so quickly run to a temple and lay prostrate before a god of stone. But they *will* run to entertainment. The word *entertain* is of Latin origin; the root words *inter* means among, and *tenir* means to hold. Collectively, *entertain* means to hold intertwined. To keep occupied and keep the attention of your thoughts in his captivity. This, my friend, is worship.

Though I'm not suggesting all entertainment is of this origin, I am saying that in this hour we must have our eyes attuned to the discernment God has given us. The enemy has captivated a generation, and through cleverly articulated stories and songs, he has intertwined their hearts, unknowingly, to his idolatry and worship. It's time he be torn down.

A CIVILIZATION POSSESSED

In 1958, Steven Engel pursued the State of New York in a lawsuit, along with other enraged parents, in a group effort to remove prayer from schools across the United States. These parents argued their case, that a prayer recitation in schools promoted religion by the state. Though their case initially fell, it was reopened, interestingly, in the early 1960s. You may remember, this was a time that was also converging with the removal of the patriarchy, the family unit, and the passageway for feminism and what would later become, the edict of death through Roe v. Wade in the early '70s.

Did it all start here, though? I believe these were the initiation years. The "sweeping clean" of the house of America that would open the doors to demons far more sinister than those of its prior history. Given how dark some of the history of the early 1900s was in terms of the horrors of slavery and the years before through the grave injustices against the Native Americans, the demons, though ominous and insidious, were about to bring with them demons seven times more wicked and devious than they. Steven Engel and his comrades would eventually go on to win their case, instigating the first of many removals of the presiding presence and protection of God in the land over the coming years. Though it was a prayer offered to the children by choice, this was deemed a violation of the establishment of the First Amendment. They essentially opened a door and cast God out of the classrooms of America's children… leaving the door ajar, however.

In the expansion of this one ruling, another case was ruled on one year later, and Bible readings and Bibles too were swiftly shown the exit door from the foundations of education in children's schools across the United States. Interestingly the case of Engel v. Vitale has prophetic meanings hidden within their names that speak of what was chosen this day. *Engel* means "messenger," and *Vitale* means "life." America chose the *messenger* of the enemy, Ishtar, and drove out *life* from the house of the United States. Jesus speaks of the principle of what took place in the 1960s in His parable in Matthew 12:43-45 (CSB):

> *When an unclean spirit comes out of a person, it roams through waterless places looking for rest but doesn't find any. Then it says, "I'll go back to my house that I came from." Returning, it finds the house vacant, swept, and put in order. Then it goes and brings with it seven other spirits more evil than itself, and they enter and settle down there. As a result, that person's last condition is worse than the first. That's how it will also be with this evil generation.*

Jonathan Cahn offers some incredible insight into this parable, where he writes in his book, *The Return of the Gods:*

> It would seem that the parable is talking about a possessed and delivered man who then becomes repossessed. It certainly could be applied to a possessed individual. But the parable is actually not about the man at all. It is only an illustration, an example, an analogy used to reveal a spiritual principle and give a prophetic warning.
>
> The key comes in the last words of the parable. After stating that the "last state of that man is worse than the first," Jesus adds, "So shall it also be with this wicked generation." Thus the parable is not about individual possession but collective, or mass, possession, the possession of a generation, a culture, a civilization. The parables immediate application appears to be the generation that lived in first-century Judea. But the principles revealed in the parable extend far beyond the age and borders of that nation. They apply to Western civilization as a whole and span the entire age into the modern world. How so? Two thousand years ago the Roman Empire and Western Civilization comprised a house of spirits, a civilization possessed of gods and spirits. But into that house came the Word of God, the Spirit of God, the gospel. Western civilization was thus set free from the spirits and became, as in the parable, a house set in order, a civilization cleansed.

Jonathan then writes, "And therein lies the warning. The house that is cleansed and put in order but remains empty will be repossessed. And if it should be repossessed, it will end up in a worse state than if it had never been cleansed."

Has the United States of America, and subsequently the nations of the earth, become possessed with demonic principalities in these days because we have failed to keep God within the boundaries and borders of our homes and nations? Have we become complacent in driving out demon principalities, making remarks like, "What can I do? We're in the last days anyway, what is the point?" If I may be so bold to say, Jesus is not returning for a weak and pathetic bride, He is returning for a glorious and victorious one.

Mordecai, as we know, is the prophetic picture of Jesus. He is the uncle who urges Esther, "You cannot stand by and be silent, this is the moment for which you have been called." Mordecai does not allow Esther to bury her head in the sand; instead, he draws out of her the shining light that she is, and calls her to attention. In a clarion call of urgency, he causes her to stand up and fight to drive out the demons in their land.

Have we swept the house clean, and then left the doors wide open to every demonic principality and prevailing spirit? Perhaps so, but could this be the hour of cleansing? A cleansing that not only drives out every demon force in our path, but *fills* the house—our houses, our homes, our cities and our nations—with the permeating presence of the Holy Spirit? This time we cannot just drive out the demons, we must *fill the house with His glory*. Esther, or Hadassah, becomes a picture of the myrtle tree covering the booths of our homes, cities and nations.

CRUSHING THE SERPENT

I have shown you the meaning of Mordecai in Hebrew, which means "to be crushed and oppressed," but we have yet to discuss the Persian translation of his name, "follower or servant of Marduk," or, "belonging to Marduk." This is a complete contradiction to who Mordecai is in Scripture. So then, who is Marduk? And why the contradiction within Mordecai's name?

We must first find out who Marduk is to obtain a fuller picture of what this means in the context of Esther and the Esther Mantle for our modern day. Marduk is a false god and was worshipped in Mesopotamian times as the chief god of Babylon. While this principality is mentioned only once in Scripture, historical records show that he was considered a chief deity, attached to not only Baal, but also Ishtar. Remember Ishtar from Chapter 5? Yes, her. These two gods, or rather principalities, were considered lovers—they were intertwined together and worked in unison to achieve their goals of domination. Which is profound in context, given that Ishtar is the counterfeit of Esther—and Marduk, the counterfeit of Mordecai.

I have no intention of leading you into an exhaustive history lesson of these demonic deities, yet it's important we understand that we are indeed dealing with these same principalities at work today. When the house of America was swept clean in the '60s, demons seven times worse than the ones before came and possessed the land, and among those, alongside Baal, Haman, and Ishtar, was Marduk. How do I know? Look for the rotting fruit. When you pick up an apple from the ground of the tree it has fallen from, even if it is rotten, you know by the fruit that it's from an apple tree. In the same way, we can distinguish the rotting stench that comes from these principalities, and thus determine God's solutions against them.

Marduk is known as the god of justice. I want you to contemplate this for a moment and think upon the correlations with the prevailing declarations of "justice" that have become dividing conversations of our day. In 2020, we began to see a steady rise in "social justice" issues. While many of these issues have a resemblance of injustice, justice through the principality of Marduk is sought through violence.

The issue of racism, for example, is a demonic injustice that certainly needs divine intervention, that needs true healing and true repentance. However, what we have seen is the manipulation through the principality of Marduk, where justice is fought for racism through further injustice and violence. This was evident in 2020 through the riots of Black Lives Matter (BLM). Was there a measure of truth to their cause? Indeed, there is still prevailing and satanic racism in our world today that we cannot tolerate, however, true and godly justice will not come by the way of more violence. May I propose, as we are constantly being divided by difference in color, there need be only one color we focus our attention on for healing and that is the color of the Blood of Jesus. It is only within His Blood that true healing and justice can come. I digress. Interestingly, the ancient depictions of this demon lord Marduk were often illustrated alongside a dragon with a forked tongue. What does a forked tongue represent? Deceit and division. Marduk merely uses injustice as a tool to create further division.

When you also consider that satan himself is depicted as a dragon serpent in Revelation, you begin to understand the severity of the nature of this principality. Furthermore, the Ishtar Gate in ancient Babylon (a gate where processions of sacrifice and pride would pass through; how profound when considering "pride parades"), featured a dragon associated with the god Marduk. This tells us that both Ishtar and Marduk have a gate through which they receive their sacrifices and idol worship. What is that gate? I believe it has come primarily through education and the idolization and worship of *enter*-tainment, which holds one in containment.

I mentioned the *Barbie* movie at the beginning of this chapter for a reason. After watching it, the Holy Spirit led me to look up the name meaning of "Mattel"—the toy company that birthed and branded Barbie. Interestingly, yet another collision into the 1960s. *Mattel* amazingly means "follower of Marduk." It is the identical meaning of Mordecai's Persian translation. While I'm not demonizing the brand itself, toys, or even the people who work at such companies, I am indeed highlighting that these demon principalities have entered the gates of our own homes, cities, and nations through seemingly innocent entryways. Does this mean you must throw out all your children's toys? By no means.

However, I believe the Lord is calling us up to higher levels of discernment in this hour, for we are the gatekeepers of our homes for our children and their futures. Just as the wolf dressed in Grandmother's clothing, these principalities have disguised themselves as fun and carefree, and placed themselves in positions of worship as such. The origins of the Barbie doll come from the inspiration of a German doll named Bild Lilli. The German word *bild* translates to mean "picture." *Lilli* means "purity." Combined, the doll's name means "picture of purity." This original doll, from which Barbie was derived and inspired, was in actuality a sex doll. Lilli dolls were sold in tobaccos shops, adult-themed toy stores, and bars with their primary consumers being grown men. Bild Lillis were used as suggestive sex toys for men at bachelor parties, bought as gag gifts for one another, and positioned in sexual and provocative ways.

Did the principality of Marduk utilize this injustice of Bild Lilli to infiltrate the apparent justice of feminism through Barbie? Maybe. Encouraging little girls to "make their dreams come true" is by no means a bad thing; but as Solomon said so wisely it is *"the little foxes that spoil the vineyards"* (Song of Solomon 2:15 CSB). This leads us to the subtle and cunning origins of a doll that would infiltrate the homes of countless little girls in the years to come. A doll that was initially suggestive and provocative, the picture of counterfeit purity, that would prophetically speaking become the picture of Ishtar.

What's more, in the movie's opening scene mentioned earlier, you will find another point of the enemy's hidden messaging when the towering idol of Barbie stands above the little girls. She is wearing the first outfit from the first creation of Barbie, the black and white striped swimsuit that was also an initial design of Bild Lilli.

Some could say I'm reaching with these details, but I find them to be of no coincidence. How does a doll that was modeled off the design of a sexual perversion become the main toy of affection for little girls in homes worldwide? A doll, whose name, Barbie, means "stranger." When you consider it all, you realize just how deceptively the enemy works. We invited a stranger into the home—a stranger with obvious markers of demonic deity. Then came the highest grossing movie of 2023. It's subtle messages should not, therefore, be ignored.

Where does this leave Mordecai? His name depicts the demonic principality of Marduk. One thing I have noticed about the Lord is that He loves to mock the enemy at his own game. Just as we saw with Haman when he was hung upon a tree, in what would be a prophetic illustration of the complete defeat of the enemy through the Cross, and now too, through Mordecai. His name, as we know, also means "crushed and oppressed." This was hidden messaging through the Father that Jesus would crush and oppress the oppressor.

Through the Cross, Jesus would become the crusher of Marduk. The adjective *mar* from which the name Mordecai is derived, is also the exact same adjective that the name Mary comes from. Mary, being the mother of Jesus, would also crush the head of the serpent, through the conception and birth of the Messiah, as was prophesied over her: *"I will put hostility between you* [the serpent] *and the woman, and between your offspring and her offspring. He will strike your head, and you will strike his heel"* (Genesis 3:15 CSB).

Is it any wonder, then, that much of the warfare we see playing out in civilization is aimed at the woman? Through extreme feminism, abortion, abuse, and today the attempt to completely deconstruct what it is to even be a woman, the enemy has been on a warpath. Mordecai not only points to the Cross, but to the woman who would crush satan as well. Perhaps no other character in the Bible, apart from Jesus Himself, champions the daughters the way Mordecai champions Esther. Jesus, too, was a beautiful uplifter of His daughters, and reveals to us that in the last days, the mantle of Esther is not only needed, but imperative for the hour at hand. It's time to crush the head of the serpent under our feet.

CLEANSING THE HOUSE

In the final chapters of the book of Esther, we find Mordecai moving in true justice, not the counterfeit kind of Marduk—but the kind that can only come through Jesus. In Esther 9:5-10 (CSB), we find that following Mordecai's decree:

> The Jews put all their enemies to the sword, killing and destroying them. They did what they pleased to those who hated them. In the fortress of Susa, the Jews killed and destroyed five hundred men, including Parshandatha, Dalphon, Aspatha, Poratha, Adalia, Aridatha, Parmashta, Arisai, Aridai, and Vaizatha. They killed these ten sons of Haman son of Hammedatha, the enemy of the Jews. However, they did not seize any plunder.

The Jews cleansed their "houses," their neighborhoods, and their city, from these demon principalities. Not only Haman alone, they also wiped out and cleaned out his entire household. His sons' names collectively mean "superior, son of the atmosphere, free and crafty, swift of the arrow. With a strong mind, he frustrates and stores for himself, the vital forces of man." Following their deaths, the king says to Esther, "In the fortress of Susa the Jews have killed and destroyed five hundred me, including Haman's ten sons. What have they done in the rest of the royal provinces? Whatever you ask *will be given to you. Whatever you seek will also be done"* (Esther 9:12 CSB).

This is prophetic of Jesus's declaration to us today, *"Ask, and it will be given to you; seek and you will find; knock and the door will be opened to you"* (Matthew 7:7 NIV). What are you asking for today, daughter? Are you asking for simple requests, or are you asking for the heads of these principalities on a platter?

Esther's reply was this, *"If it pleases the king, may the Jews who are in Susa also have tomorrow to carry out today's law, and may the bodies of Haman's ten sons be hung on the gallows"* (Esther 9:13 CSB).

> *So the king commanded that this be done. An edict was issued in Susa, and they hanged the ten sons of Haman. On the fourteenth day of the month of Adar, the Jews in Susa came together again and put to death three hundred men there, but they did not lay a hand on the plunder. The rest of the Jews in the royal provinces also assembled to defend themselves and rid themselves of their enemies. They killed 75,000 who hated them, but they did not lay a hand on the plunder* (**Esther 9:14-16 BSB**).

You may recall, that Haman had built a gallows 75 feet tall to hang Mordecai and the Jews upon. Is it any coincidence then, that they killed 75,000 of their enemies? I believe this was intentional of God—the very thing Haman had set out to make as a declaration, God turned into His own declaration over their enemies. The Jews destroyed them.

Today, we could say that we have hundreds of thousands of demonic enemies (spiritually speaking). What if we too are called to destroy these demons from our homes, cities, and nations? It's worth noting, too, that they did not lay a hand on the plunder of their enemies. We need to be aware of this—we cannot engage with the plunder of the enemies in our day. In other words, we must let their fruit fall to the ground and rot; we don't try and rebirth their idolatry into something new.

Then we find that Esther asked of the king for the rotting bodies of Haman's house. She commanded that they, too, be hung on the tree that Haman was put to death on. She cleaned house, and then declared to the principalities—you've lost. In yet another prophetic act, she showed us how to overcome this principality—we overcome by the Cross, by the Blood of the Lamb that dripped from the tree. Do you remember how the same word for gallows, *ets,* is tree? Haman and his sons were a foreshadow of the complete victory over satan and *all* his demon deities—every last one of them.

DISMANTLING PRINCIPALITIES AND MANTLING ESTHER

Mordecai and Esther together send out a final letter with full authority from the king to confirm the days of Purim, which was the celebration of the victory over Haman and their enemies.

> *For this reason these days are called Purim, from the word pur. Because of all the instructions in this letter as well as what they had witnessed and what had*

happened to them, the Jews bound themselves, their descendants, and all who joined with them to a commitment that they would not fail to celebrate these two days each and every year according to the written instructions and according to the time appointed. These days are remembered and celebrated by every generation, family, province, and city, so that they days of Purim will not lose their significance in Jewish life and their memory will not fade from their descendants. Queen Esther, daughter of Abihail, along with Mordecai the Jew, wrote this second letter with full authority to confirm the letter about Purim. He sent letters with assurances of peace and security to all the Jews who were in the 127 provinces of the kingdom of Ahasuerus, in order to confirm these days of Purim at their proper time just as Mordecai the Jew and Esther the queen had established them and just as they had committed themselves and their descendants to the practices of fasting and lamentation (**Esther 9:26-31 CSB**).

There are a number of things to note here, Esther and Mordecai called this celebration of remembrance *Purim*, which, as you may recall means "to dismantle and divide," and it reveals the checkmate Haman had fallen into. The very thing he used to destroy them became the name of their victory for years and generations to come. Through the Father and the rending of their hearts, Esther and Mordecai saw firsthand the effects of God, the Father of strength (Abihail), move in response to their cries.

I believe this speaks to us today of God, our Father of strength moving in power over our enemies to cut and divide them, as we rend our hearts before Him for the sake of these generations. Oh, that we would weep before Him for the lost of our day today, for the ones who have been cast under the decree of death set by Haman and other demonic entities. Oh, that we would cry out before the Lord and lay down the idols of our day and plead His Blood over the sins of the land. Oh, that we would drive out the idols, that we would refuse fellowship with them and be a bride purified, in readiness for our King.

Do you recall Zeresh? Haman's wife? Her name means "golden star of adoration." We have looked upon the stars of Hollywood with adoration, upon the stars of the earth with all its fame and glitter, as some glorious thing to behold. When in reality, it's nothing more than the falling stars of death. That's not to say that there are not sons and daughters working within it to purify it, for we have many friends who are shining lights within its darkness. What I'm saying is, I believe we are on the precipice of a mighty shift upon the earth where the stars of Haman, Zeresh, Ishtar, and Marduk will fall.

I would go so far to say, even, within the body of Christ. For we too have treated leaders, worship leaders, and influencers within the church as famed celebrities that we gush over in idolatrous ways. I believe in honoring those who lead us, and I have great honor and respect for those who lead pathways before us. Yet, my adoration and worship is reserved only for Jesus.

I also believe the Lord is purifying His bride in this hour. Gone are the days of the worship of stars, for we will behold the face of just one Star—the true Morning Star, yes, even as we carry the mantle of Esther. My prayer is that the only Star we would behold would be Jesus. Even as we shine for Him as stars, it would never be to reflect upon ourselves, but only to make Him more known. (Mordecai is famous and known.) I believe in these last days, we will see many "stars" fade, many who have adored and loved the fame and celebrity culture of adoration that has plagued the landscape of the body of Christ for too long.

God is exposing the works of glitter for the bitter dust that it actually is. He isn't interested in a bride that is prideful and points all to herself. He is pursuing the heart of a bride who will surrender every aspect of her life and shine beautifully only for Him. Isn't it stunningly poetic that the book of Esther finishes in chapter 10, detailing the accounts of Mordecai's great rank with which the king had honored him, and how his fame and esteem grew among the people. The book of Esther is complete with the rising fame of Mordecai—the foreshadow of the rising fame of Jesus.

Esther, too, finds her completion in Jesus, for I must show you one final detail about her. Her Hebrew name, Hadassah, comes from the root word *hadam,* which means "footstool." Psalm 110:1 the New Living Translation declares: *"The Lord said to my Lord, 'Sit in the place of honor at my right hand until I humble your enemies, making them a footstool under your feet.'"* Do you recall one of the name meanings of Mordecai is "son of the right hand"? Could this verse alone stand as a complete picture of what God longs to write through you as you carry the mantle of Esther with Jesus today? Where He will make your enemies a footstool under your feet?

You have been mantled, daughter, to take down the giants of the land. Now, go, for the hour is short, the time is critical, and your voice must arise. Go and shine like a star with the light of His glory into every dark place on the earth. Go into your homes, go into the schools, universities, industries of every kind; go into the governments and media; go into the high places and declare this new edict: "The Blood of Jesus speaks a better word." Then tear down the idols, drive out and annihilate the demons. It's time to ready yourself as a pure bride filled with the oil of His presence. It's time to shine for His glory—for such a time as this—that He may return to a victorious church with the serpent under our feet.

THE MAN AMONG THE MYRTLE TREES

In one final detail, I want to show you the exquisite picture of the end-times bride, the bride of Jesus, mantled with the anointing of Esther in these last days. It's found in Zechariah 1:8-11 (NIV), where Zechariah describes his vision:

> During the night I had a vision, and there before me was a man mounted on a red horse. He was standing among the myrtle trees in a ravine. Behind him were red, brown and white horses. I asked, "What are these, my lord?" The angel who was talking with me answered, "I will show you what they are." Then the man standing among the myrtle trees explained, "They are the ones the Lord has sent to go throughout the earth." And they reported to the angel of the Lord who was standing among the myrtle trees, "We have gone throughout the earth and found the whole world at rest and in peace.

I found the following commentary by Charles Spurgeon particularly beautiful, in light of the Esther Mantle:

> The vision in this chapter describes the condition of Israel in Zechariah's day; but being interpreted in its aspect towards us, it describes the Church of God as we find it now in the world. The Church is compared to a myrtle grove flourishing in a valley. It is hidden, unobserved, secreted; courting no honour and attracting no observation from the careless gazer. The Church, like her head, has a glory, but it is concealed from carnal eyes, for the time of her breaking forth in all her splendour is not yet come. The idea of tranquil security is also suggested to us: for the myrtle grove in the valley is still and calm, while the storm sweeps over the mountain summits. Tempests spend their force upon the craggy peaks of the Alps, but down yonder where flows the stream which maketh glad the city of our God, the myrtles flourish by the still waters, all unshaken by the impetuous wind. How great is the inward tranquility of God's Church! Even when opposed and persecuted, she has a peace which the world gives not, and which, therefore, it cannot take away: the peace of God which passeth all understanding keeps the hearts and minds of God's people. Does not the metaphor forcibly picture the peaceful, perpetual growth of the saints? The myrtle sheds not her leaves, she is always green; and the Church in her worst time still hath a blessed verdure of grace about her; nay, she has sometimes exhibited most verdure

when her winter has been sharpest. She has prospered most when her adversities have been most severe. Hence the text hints at victory. The myrtle is the emblem of peace, and a significant token of triumph. The brows of conquerors were bound with myrtle and with laurel; and is not the Church ever victorious? Is not every Christian more than a conqueror through him that loved him? Living in peace, do not the saints fall asleep in the arms of victory?

—Charles Spurgeon[1]

Dare I say, that the hour has now come for the revealing of the true bride of Jesus mantled in the anointing of Esther. She is the grove of myrtle trees among which Jesus, the Man among them, is standing. This is such a beautiful portrait—Jesus, our Mordecai, upon His victory horse, standing among His victorious bride of Queen Esthers. Could the horses be speaking of the bride as well? The red, brown, and white horses, all pointing to the redemptive colors of the Cross: red and brown pointing to His blood, and white declaring of the purification that will come as we release Him to the earth. Could the horses be representing the body of Christ as messengers to be sent around the earth with the powerful and victorious weapon of the Blood? I believe so.

You see, everything about Esther points to Jesus and His finished work, and these verses paint for us the finality of the mantle. Our strategy in this hour is to ride upon the power of the finished work of the Cross. We will run and not grow weary; we will walk and not become faint. We will make our enemies our footstools.

Are you ready daughter? It's time to mount up and ride—it's time to pour out the oil of healing upon the lands and release the power of the Blood of the Lamb.

NOTE

1. Jason K. Allen, "Lord's Day Meditation: The Myrtle Trees That Were in the Bottom" by C.H. Spurgeon, May 5, 2018; from Spurgeon's *Evening and Morning Devotions,* September 26; https://jasonkallen .com/2018/05/lords-day-meditation-the-myrtle-trees-that-were-in -the-bottom-by-c-h-spurgeon/; accessed April 15, 2024.

ABOUT CHRISTY JOHNSTON

Christy Johnston is an intercessor, teacher, prophetic voice, and justice carrier. Christy's burning heart for justice and intercession has led her on a life journey of prayer, contending for major world issues. Together with her husband, Nate, and their three daughters, Charlotte, Sophie, and Ava, Christy lives in Australia while contending for both their home country and North America. She is passionate to raise and empower God's sons and daughters to release the Kingdom of God around the world.

From

CHRISTY JOHNSTON

Access Heaven's Solutions For Every Problem and Crisis That You Face in Life!

The mystery of the Kingdom is that, through our prophetic prayers and decrees, we can partner with God to change our world.

Seasoned prophetic intercessor, Christy Johnston, shares the revelation she received when God intervened in her life by revealing supernatural strategies to the struggles she was facing. As Christy partnered with what God was showing her, she was emboldened to pray in another dimension—a realm of Kingdom authority that sees answered prayers and circumstances shift. You have access to this realm!

Watch God transform your world as you partner with Him in prophetic prayer!

Purchase your copy wherever books are sold.

From

NATE JOHNSTON

Wild Ones, Arise!

There is a move of God that is stirring and a remnant has heard the call—wild, radical lovers of Jesus that have been hidden for far too long. Once the burnt out. The outcast. The voiceless and muzzled. Now they arise as the burning ones to release the word of the Lord and fire of Heaven into the four corners of the earth. They are the carriers of reformation, revival, and unique and undignified movements. They are a generation of David's called for such a time as this.

In *The Wild Ones*, prophet and worship leader Nate Johnston offers an urgent summons to the wilderness prophetic voices, and a jarring wakeup call to the established church: If we are to experience a fresh outpouring of the Spirit, we must reform!

In this timely book, Nate offers prophetic insights and Biblical revelation that will set you free from the fear of man, bring a fresh download from Heaven, and reveal your place in God's agenda to bring Heaven to Earth!

Now is the time to emerge from the wilderness and be the new sound and voice of truth that will unshackle bonds of oppression, remove veils, and set the captives free.

Purchase your copy wherever books are sold.